INSIDE THE MINDS

# Working with Government Agencies in Tax Law

*Leading Lawyers on Staying Up-to-Date on New Tax Laws, Understanding the Roles of Key Players in Tax Investigations, and Avoiding Trouble Spots for Corporate Clients*



ASPATORE

Mat #40772644

# BOOK & ARTICLE IDEA SUBMISSIONS

If you are a C-Level executive, senior lawyer, or venture capitalist interested in submitting a book or article idea to the Aspatore editorial board for review, please e-mail TLR.AspatoreAuthors@thomson.com. Aspatore is especially looking for highly specific ideas that would have a direct financial impact on behalf of a reader. Completed publications can range from 2 to 2,000 pages. Include your book/article idea, biography, and any additional pertinent information.



*Inside the Minds* Project Manager, Caitlin Keiper; edited by Michaela Falls; proofread by Melanie Zimmerman



---

ISBN 978-0-314-19908-9

For corrections, updates, comments or any other inquiries please e-mail
TLR.AspatoreEditorial@thomson.com.

First Printing, 2008
10 9 8 7 6 5 4 3 2 1

---

## Praise for *Inside the Minds*

"Need-to-read inside information and analysis that will improve your bottom line - the best source in the business." – Daniel J. Moore, Member, Harris Beach LLP

"The Inside the Minds series is a valuable probe into the thought, perspectives, and techniques of accomplished professionals…" – Chuck Birenbaum, Partner, Thelen Reid & Priest

"Aspatore has tapped into a gold mine of knowledge and expertise ignored by other publishing houses." – Jack Barsky, Managing Director, Information Technology & Chief Information Officer, ConEdison *Solutions*

"Unlike any other publisher – actual authors that are on the front-lines of what is happening in industry." – Paul A. Sellers, Executive Director, National Sales, Fleet and Remarketing, Hyundai Motor America

"A snapshot of everything you need..." – Charles Koob, Co-Head of Litigation Department, Simpson Thacher & Bartlet

"Everything good books should be - honest, informative, inspiring, and incredibly well-written." – Patti D. Hill, President, BlabberMouth PR

"Great information for both novices and experts." – Patrick Ennis, Partner, ARCH Venture Partners

"A rare peek behind the curtains and into the minds of the industry's best." – Brandon Baum, Partner, Cooley Godward

"Intensely personal, practical advice from seasoned dealmakers." – Mary Ann Jorgenson, Coordinator of Business Practice Area, Squire, Sanders & Dempsey

"Great practical advice and thoughtful insights." – Mark Gruhin, Partner, Schmeltzer, Aptaker & Shepard, PC

"Reading about real-world strategies from real working people beats the typical business book hands down." - Andrew Ceccon, Chief Marketing Officer, OnlineBenefits Inc.

"Books of this publisher are syntheses of actual experiences of real-life, hands-on, front-line leaders--no academic or theoretical nonsense here. Comprehensive, tightly organized, yet nonetheless motivational!" - Lac V. Tran, Sr. Vice President, CIO and Associate Dean Rush University Medical Center

"Aspatore is unlike other publishers…books feature cutting-edge information provided by top executives working on the front-line of an industry." - Debra Reisenthel, President and CEO, Novasys Medical Inc

ASPATORE

## www.Aspatore.com

Aspatore Books, a Thomson Reuters business, is the largest and most exclusive publisher of C-level executives (CEO, CFO, CTO, CMO, partner) from the world's most respected companies and law firms. Aspatore annually publishes a select group of C-level executives from the Global 1,000, top 250 law firms (partners and chairs), and other leading companies of all sizes. C-Level Business Intelligence™, as conceptualized and developed by Aspatore Books, provides professionals of all levels with proven business intelligence from industry insiders—direct and unfiltered insight from those who know it best—as opposed to third-party accounts offered by unknown authors and analysts. Aspatore Books is committed to publishing an innovative line of business and legal books, those which lay forth principles and offer insights that, when employed, can have a direct financial impact on the reader's business objectives, whatever they may be. In essence, Aspatore publishes critical tools—need-to-read as opposed to nice-to-read books—for all business professionals.

## Inside the Minds

The critically acclaimed *Inside the Minds* series provides readers of all levels with proven business intelligence from C-level executives (CEO, CFO, CTO, CMO, partner) from the world's most respected companies. Each chapter is comparable to a white paper or essay and is a future-oriented look at where an industry/profession/topic is heading and the most important issues for future success. Each author has been selected based upon their experience and C-level standing within the professional community. *Inside the Minds* was conceived in order to give readers actual insights into the leading minds of business executives worldwide. Because so few books or other publications are actually written by executives in industry, *Inside the Minds* presents an unprecedented look at various industries and professions never before available.

# CONTENTS

# Achieving Success for Corporate Clients in Tax Investigations

Armando Gomez

*Partner*

Skadden, Arps, Slate, Meagher & Flom LLP

ASPATORE

As a tax attorney, I spend most of my time representing large companies in several types of situations, including IRS audits of novel or otherwise significant transactions, internal investigations involving tax matters, and governmental investigations of tax matters, which can arise through the Justice Department or U.S. Attorney's Offices, and in some cases through Congress.

I believe that I bring the most value to my clients by helping them to navigate the IRS system, and also by helping them to manage their way through controversies and investigations, which can often be quite difficult to resolve, as they usually involve either significant dollars or significant reputation risk—or both. Not only are the tax people at the client company involved in these investigations, but usually senior management and, in some cases, their boards of directors are involved as well, and they all need to pay close attention to what is going on, as these are high stakes situations.

## Mistakes to Avoid

Certainly, one of the most common mistakes I have seen in this area occurs when companies rush to defend themselves by essentially saying, "We are right and the government is wrong." On a number of occasions, I have seen companies instinctively take the position that the government should not be taking the time to investigate a certain situation—but such attitudes are not conducive to winning over government investigators. If you approach a government investigation in a self-righteous manner, all that you likely will end up doing is causing the government agency to want to dig in more. Of course, this is obvious, common sense advice, but it is the type of lesson that all too often is not learned until it is too late to avoid being embroiled in a really big mess

Another mistake companies often make occurs when they rush to go over an investigator's head; they may try to call the top person in a government organization in an attempt to ask them to "call off the dogs," and while there are certainly some times when that is an appropriate action to take, you usually should not do so on the very first day of an investigation.

## Key Federal Agencies That Enforce Tax Law

Federal tax law is developed by two key entities—Congress and the Treasury Department. Tax-related investigations can originate from three places—the IRS, the Department of Justice, and Congress, because there are congressional committees that spend a lot of time investigating tax matters. Enforcement is primarily the province of the IRS and the Department of Justice, to some extent.

I have found that the IRS and the Department of Justice tend to work closely together in terms of enforcement. Both focus on trying to collect the tax dollars they think are due. However, as probably occurs in any type of advocacy situation, the zeal with which the government pursues a particular case where they believe that a company or individual taxpayer has underpaid their taxes often causes the government to lose sight of the consequences of the actions they are taking. In some cases, an enforcement agency may wind up creating new tax law through their efforts to win one particular case—and that law may be at odds with the laws that Congress and the Treasury Department have been trying to develop elsewhere. For example, one of the more notorious tax shelters of recent times, which is often referred to as the "son-of-boss" shelter, was developed by clever lawyers who figured out that the conclusion reached by the United States Tax Court in a case decided in favor of the IRS in 1976 might be applied in a way favorable to taxpayers when the shelters were sold. The government ended up spending considerable resources to challenge this shelter, and promulgated regulations to reverse the rule adopted back in 1976. In a less notorious area, in July 2007 the IRS announced that it would no longer contest the treatment of cash advances received by grocery stores from suppliers with whom the stores entered into volume purchase commitments, only to learn the next day that the United States Court of Appeals for the Third Circuit had ruled in favor of the IRS on that very issue. (Although the Court had been informed of the IRS's announcement, because the Department of Justice did not advise the Court that it was changing its litigating position, the Court proceeded to issue its opinion.) *See Karn's Prime & Fancy Food Ltd. v. Commissioner*, 494 F.3d 404 (3rd Cir. 2007).

## Staying Up to Date with the New Tax Laws

There are two key aspects involved in staying up to date with current tax law. First, it is important to know how the regulatory organizations work, and that is something that you learn by doing. However, the tax laws and rules change on a frequent basis, and there are very few people who could legitimately say that they are familiar with all the rules—and I am certainly not one of them. Therefore, I try to keep up to date in the areas where I focus in my practice, and that process involves a lot of reading and homework.

Fortunately, as tax law has developed, the Treasury Department has done a good job of communicating those new rules and regulations, both in their official releases, as well as through press conferences and speeches, and the regulators make an effort to let people know what issues they are evaluating, while soliciting input from the business community. However, the government does not tend to share as much information with respect to enforcement strategies, which is to be expected.

Of course, it is not just keeping abreast of developments in the law that is important, but also keeping up on what issues the IRS is focused on in their examinations. Some of this is information that can be found through the IRS's Web site, as they publicize key issues of interest in their examinations. *See* http://www.irs.gov/businesses/article/0,,id=167377,00.html.

However, it is often developments in the business world that lead to new IRS controversies and areas of audit focus. For example, in early 2006 a series of news reports on the topic of possible stock option backdating lead to a number of government probes around the country, and many companies conducted internal investigations on this topic because of the publicity around this issue. A number of significant tax issues could arise in the context of backdated stock options, but this was not really a well-developed area of the law at the time because very few people had ever given serious thought to the issue. As a result, tax lawyers advising companies on these issues had to try to sort through these rules at the same time that the IRS was conducting audits and trying to develop their own interpretations.

## The Roles of Government Agencies in Tax Investigations

If a client is involved in an ordinary audit, it is the IRS that performs the investigatory work. The IRS has teams of revenue agents with extensive resources. They will go through the relevant papers that the taxpayer is asked to provide; analyze the information that the documentation contains; and then deal directly with the taxpayer or their adviser to develop their case. The IRS has their own lawyers that support them throughout this administrative phase, which is handled internally. If the IRS proposes tax adjustments and the taxpayer doesn't agree with them, the taxpayer usually can request a second look through the IRS Office of Appeals. It is only at the end of these processes that taxpayers typically have to confront the question of whether to concede the adjustments or contest them in the courts.

The tax world is somewhat unique in that you usually get to pick which court in which to litigate with the IRS. Many taxpayers go to the United States Tax Court, because you do not have to pay the tax first in order to contest an IRS assessment in that forum. The Tax Court is made up of judges who only consider tax cases, and many of the judges came from long careers at the IRS, Department of Justice, or tax practice. Taxpayers interested in taking their case to a jury or a local judge will often go to the Federal District Court where they are located, and other taxpayers will choose to litigate in the Court of Federal Claims, which is a specialized court that generally hears tax and patent cases. However, if a taxpayer wants to litigate in the Federal District Court or Court of Federal Claims, the price of admission is to pay the disputed tax and then sue for a refund. Depending on the amount at stake, this can sometimes influence the choice of forum equation.

The choice of forum question also affects who the lawyers will be on the other side. In cases before the United States Tax Court, the IRS is represented by its own lawyers; in the other federal courts, the IRS is represented by lawyers from the Department of Justice. The discovery rules and procedures tend to differ between the courts as well, so taxpayers have to consider a number of factors when evaluating these decisions.

When a case involves potentially criminal matters, taxpayers will be dealing with either the criminal investigative division of the IRS or the Department of Justice. It is usually obvious when you are in one of these situations, or when you may be in what we refer to as an "eggshell audit," where the tax lawyer's job is to try to convince the government to keep the matter on the "civil side of the house."

However, over the last decade several situations have arisen wherein a number of federal agencies came together in a joint law enforcement effort, sometimes very quickly. One of the first and most prominent of those situations was the Enron case, where the government created a task force comprised of professionals from the FBI, SEC, IRS, and other agencies, all working together. Although the primary focus in such investigations may start with securities law or other non-tax issues, once the IRS is brought into the picture companies need to make sure that they are handling their response to the investigation in a way that takes into account all of the many possible tax aspects—and that means making sure that they have a team of lawyers with expertise in all of these different areas.

A more recent enforcement situation that ultimately involved hundreds of companies was the phenomenon of backdated stock options. As noted above, this issue received a significant amount of press coverage starting early in 2006. First a handful of companies and then hundreds of companies were investigated by the SEC, Department of Justice, and the IRS. Many people initially thought that backdated stock options was a securities law issue, but it also turned out there were some very significant tax issues involved in this situation. For example, companies that issued so-called "incentive stock options" (ISOs) quickly discovered that the options couldn't qualify as ISOs if they had been issued at a discount. This meant that companies could be liable for penalties for failure to properly withhold taxes when the options had been exercised. An even more significant problem involved a law enacted in 2004 that was intended to deter companies from establishing certain types of deferred compensation arrangements. Although few people probably could have conceived of it at the time, the 2004 law (referred to by tax lawyers as section 409A) ended up affecting hundreds of companies that uncovered backdated or misdated stock options as a result of the investigations referenced above.

## The Role of the Tax Attorney

One mistake that many companies make when confronted with a crisis that may wind up involving considerable coordination between different federal agencies is not being cognizant of the fact that they have a tax problem. In other cases, they might know that they have a tax problem, and they choose to ignore it (perhaps thinking that it is only a tax problem and cannot possibly be as important as the other issues on which they are focused), or they do not bother to consult advisers who know how to deal with these tax issues. They may think that they would be better off trying to solve other issues that are important to them, but they will only end up with a significant IRS problem that they will have to deal with later on.

I have found that tax lawyers are most often called in when a client is involved in either a large transaction, or when they are facing a major tax issue—the resolution of which could have a very significant material effect on the company in terms of dollars at stake. For example, if a large public company has a $1 million tax problem, they are not likely going to call someone like me; they will generally handle smaller issues internally with their own internal tax professionals. However, if they have an issue involving tens of millions over a number of years, they will then enlist the services of a tax attorney. A tax attorney's counsel can also be valuable if a company is facing reputation issues—i.e., the IRS alleges that the company did something that was not just wrong, but criminal or fraudulent. When a company is facing a congressional investigation, they will often find that such an investigation is not so much a search for the truth, but a race to the newspapers. These cases often involve a fair amount of PR management, and having advisers who know how to deal with these situations is very important.

## Key Issues When Working with Agents in a Tax Investigation

When I first start to work with a client on a tax-related investigation, I typically will try to obtain as much of the facts as I can from that client up front, in order to make sure that I have a full picture of the situation. I also try to get a good sense of the most important points of concern for the client. It is also critical to determine at a very early stage which governmental entity (or entities) we are dealing with; what is the best way to approach that government agency or office; and then establish some lines of communication.

Indeed, my top priority when working on a client's tax matter is making sure that I have established good lines of communication with the governmental officials who are investigating the matter. Simply put, once you know what the client is concerned about and what they are trying to achieve, you need to establish a solid relationship with the government investigators and regulators that they are dealing with, and develop a level of trust in those communications. Ultimately, I have found that it is much easier to resolve your client's issues if you are able to establish the right type of dialogue and the right level of trust and communication with the other side. Only then will you be able to convince those regulators with respect to your client's position and achieve your client's goals.

From my perspective, the best way to reach out to these government officials is to try to avoid being the proverbial "bull in the china shop." Once you have the reputation of being that type of a player, it is very hard to eliminate that impression. Therefore, while it might feel good to pick a fight with someone in the government, it rarely pays. I know that I am going to be doing this work for a number of years—and people in the government have long memories. Therefore, I try to approach each case in the same way—by dealing with the government in a fair manner. In many cases I wind up dealing with the same people that I have dealt with previously on behalf of different clients, and fortunately, I have built and cultivated those relationships over the years in such a way that these regulators know that they can work with me and trust what I tell them.

## Developing Case Strategy

Very few of the cases I handle are anything like the ones I have handled before; each is unique. Therefore, I do not utilize a uniform set of questions or a standard checklist when I meet with a new client; the questions that I ask are always specific to the problem that the client is trying to deal with. However, the strategy that I use in each case is going to be similar in terms of making sure that I have a full picture of the facts up front, and that I identify the key goals that the client wants to achieve. For example, if the client is involved in a tax audit, our goal may be to make sure that the taxpayer's position is upheld 100 percent, or if the client is facing some litigation risk, we may try to negotiate a settlement of some sort.

Many companies, for various reasons, will be interested in resolving their issues sooner rather than later, and some companies prefer to resolve their issues administratively, without going to court, in order to ensure that the matter is kept private and does not show up in the press. Different clients will have different strategy preferences and tolerances, and some will place a premium on resolving matters quietly. Therefore, it is important to understand the key drivers for the client, because that will then influence how you approach and deal with the government.

For example, I recently handled a case for a client who had been through an audit and pursued administrative appeals within the IRS Office of Appeals, which entails going before what is essentially an equivalent of an administrative law judge, in order to try to resolve their case. These attempts had failed. However, the IRS also has a confidential arbitration program, which we went into because the client wanted to reach a resolution quickly, without a public courtroom battle. This arbitration program was one way to get to a final answer without having to go through the time, expense, and publicity associated with litigating the case in the courts, which could take two to three years from start to finish. The arbitration process took only six months. Of course, arbitration can be a risky proposition and is not for everyone. A more common approach is to pursue mediation, and the IRS has a very solid program in place that often is conducive to resolving difficult cases in a prompt, fair, and confidential manner.

## Challenges in Working with Tax Agencies

Most of these cases are challenging, largely because there is often a great deal of skepticism on the part of people in the government as to the information that is given to them; or they may believe that a certain type of transaction is inherently wrong. There is also a fair amount of turnover in the government, and in many cases you will find that the people who are working on these cases do not have as much experience as people in the private sector—although that is obviously not the fault of the government personnel assigned to the case, it can certainly impact how you are able to proceed. In these cases, there can be a challenge involved in making sure that you are effectively communicating with the person on the other side of the table. For example, you may have to educate the government official with respect to your client's issues before you can get into a discussion as to why you think the case should be resolved in a certain way.

It is difficult to avoid these challenges because they stem from external factors that are beyond anyone's control. All that you can do is to come to the table with a lot of patience, and understand that the process of resolving an issue in your client's favor is going to require a fair amount of work. You need to build a level of trust and educate the other side to either convince them that your client's position is correct—or even if it is not completely correct, that there is a reasonable solution to their problem. Of course, the lawyer also has to educate his or her client, because what may seem like a simple thing to handle can often require a significant amount of time and effort to ultimately resolve.

## The Client's Responsibilities in Working with Tax Agencies

It is essential for the client to keep in mind that most companies will deal with the IRS at some point in time; certainly, the largest companies deal with the IRS all the time. Nearly every public company I know of has office space in their headquarters occupied year round by IRS agents who are auditing that company, and those companies have in-house tax departments who deal with the IRS on a daily or weekly basis. It is important for the people who work in the client's in-house tax department to know how to coordinate their dealings with the IRS; establish a good information flow; and build the kind of relationship with IRS officials that will enable them to have a good understanding of the types of areas that the IRS will be auditing.

When the IRS asks for documents with respect to a particular issue or transaction, I have found that clients tend to respond to these requests in one of three ways. One way is to fight the IRS tooth and nail and give them the minimum amount of information. Another way is to gather as much paper as they can; dump it on the IRS; and hope they do not find anything in the midst of it all. The third way is to try to give the IRS what they ask for, and provide it to them in a way that is organized, in the hope that the

IRS will come to the conclusion that you want them to arrive at. In most cases, the only result of the first two strategies is that it will take longer for the IRS to reach the proper conclusion. Therefore, I typically encourage the people who deal with the IRS at the client company to take the third path, which I have found tends to be more conducive to leading the IRS to where you want them to go. I often tell my clients that a lot of what we do is similar to a "paint by numbers" strategy—if you can map out a path for the IRS by piecing together documentation so that the facts naturally lead from point A to point B to point C, you can reach a resolution much more quickly. Simply put, you have to package your information in a way that will lead the IRS to the conclusion that you want them to reach.

### Common Tax Violations and Investigation Timelines

All public companies get audited continually; the IRS will generally audit a large public company for up to three or four years at a time, and once they are done with the returns from those past years they will start auditing the more current returns. Indeed, if you are a big taxpayer, you are likely to be a frequent customer of the IRS, whether you like it or not. The IRS also responds to what appears in the newspapers; therefore, when the stock option backdating scandal hit the press in 2006, the IRS started looking at SEC filings, and those companies who disclosed their filing or were reported in the press to have backdated stock options started getting contacted by the IRS.

The IRS ordinarily has three years after you file your return to complete their audit. In some cases, the IRS will ask the taxpayer to extend the statute of limitations—and some companies are willing to do that, while some companies are not. However, if you do not extend the statute of limitation you will have to reach some resolution with the IRS very quickly, which may not be the resolution you want. Other companies will routinely extend the statute of limitations, and during those extra three or four years, they will try to force the IRS to move things along and wrap up their work.

Other external factors may come into play with respect to an investigation timeline. For example, if a company is facing substantial exposure in an IRS investigation, and what ultimately matters is how those numbers hit the company's financial statements, the company will often prefer to resolve the matter in a way that is going to have the smallest impact on its financial statements. Indeed, if a company is unable to book tax benefits for financial statement purposes for an extended period of time, that can be a drag on its earnings.

Another external factor on the investigation timeline occurs when companies are in the M&A market; they may either be in the midst of a big merger, or they may wish to go public or take some other major action in the marketplace. In such cases, a company will often try to clean up historic or legacy issues. For example, if a company has a number of unresolved IRS audits from eight years ago that may affect its success in a potential merger, it may try to press the IRS to get those matters resolved quickly.

**Preventative Efforts**

The best preventative effort that a company can take in an IRS audit situation is to have good documentation—and to keep careful records of what they provide to the IRS. Surprisingly, I have found that many companies do not really know what they have given the IRS; they will often tell me, "Well, we gave them all the documents that they asked for, but we don't have a copy of what we gave them." It is very difficult for a lawyer to have the full factual picture of the client's situation if they do not know what documentation has already been looked at by the agency representative who is sitting across the table.

Therefore, making sure that the company has accurate and robust document retention procedures in place is essential. There are many types of transactions where the client needs to have a complete set of documentation compiled at the time they undertake the transaction. In addition, there are many decisions that are made at the time a transaction is entered into which will prove to be critical factual issues should the transaction get audited in the future. For example, a common approach of the IRS when contesting transactions they do not like is to argue that the transaction was motivated by a sufficient "business purpose." The most convincing proof to rebut such arguments is of course the documentation from the time of the transaction that shows that the company did in fact have a compelling "business purpose" for their transaction. Therefore, it is often useful to interview some of the key businesspeople at the time you do the transaction, because by the time a certain issue gets audited several years later, the person who was involved in the matter may not work for your company anymore. In addition, an interview based on what someone remembers three to five years after the fact is not as probative of what was on their mind at the time they did the transaction. If you have the right set of interviews that were conducted at the time of the transaction, and if you have collected all of the proper documents at that point in time as well, then if you are audited you should have everything you need to defend yourself already compiled and organized.

**Final Thoughts**

In my practice, I have found that working with the government requires common sense and honesty. If I have obtained all of the key facts from my client, I know what they want to achieve. And if I have a good working relationship with the people at the IRS that the client is dealing with, then, while I might not be able to obtain the exact result that the client is looking for, I will certainly be better equipped to try to achieve that result. Success in this practice area really comes down to complete and honest communication with your client, and the appropriate level of communication with the IRS in order to get to a common sense result.

*Armando Gomez, a partner for Skadden, Arps, Slate, Meagher & Flom LLP, concentrates his practice on a broad range of tax matters. He advises clients on the structuring and financing of domestic and international partnerships and joint ventures, mergers and acquisitions, spin-offs, cross-border transactions, and foreign infrastructure projects. He also advises clients in connection with structuring private equity investments and investments in projects eligible for certain tax credits. In addition, Mr. Gomez advises clients on transfer pricing matters, at both the planning and controversy stages.*

*Mr. Gomez represents clients in federal and state tax controversy matters, including in connection with examinations and administrative appeals. He also has represented clients in summons enforcement matters and in criminal tax investigations. Mr. Gomez also advises clients in connection with internal investigations on tax-related matters.*

*Mr. Gomez represents clients in administrative and policy matters before the U.S. Department of the Treasury and the Internal Revenue Service, including commenting on regulations, tax treaties and other tax policy issues, and in connection with applications for private letter rulings.*

*Mr. Gomez also advises clients on legislative matters, including commenting on proposed legislation, developing strategies for new legislative proposals, and representing clients before the congressional tax writing committees. In this regard, Mr. Gomez has represented several clients in connection with congressional investigations, including in the largest-ever congressional investigation of a single corporate taxpayer.*

*An active member of the American Bar Association's Section of Taxation, Mr. Gomez is also a frequent lecturer and author on topics relating to partnerships and joint ventures, corporate tax shelters and related controversies and ongoing tax legislative matters.*

*Mr. Gomez received his A.B. from Duke University, his J.D. from Georgetown University Law Center, and his LL.M. from Georgetown University Law Center.*

# Dealing with State and Federal Tax Agencies

Scot C. Crow

*Partner*

Roetzel & Andress

ASPATORE

The Internal Revenue Service and the Ohio Department of Taxation are the agencies responsible for developing, investigating, and enforcing the tax laws for the federal government and the State of Ohio, where I have my practice. Typically, the navigation of tax investigations for both the state and federal tax agencies begins with the question of whether you are dealing with a civil tax issue or a criminal tax issue. I have found that the civil tax divisions for the IRS and the Ohio Department of Taxation are generally cooperative. The criminal divisions, however, tend to be less cooperative and more adversarial. The criminal tax division is a more serious matter when the IRS is building a case against the client. Both division handle all tax issues, but "fraud" is one of the trigger's to land you in the "criminal division."

The different roles that government agents have in tax investigations, enforcements, or prosecutions include that of auditors, hearing officers, enforcement agents, special enforcement divisions, and various levels of administrative positions. Simply a right to be heard, the IRS can't simply assess taxes without giving the taxpayer the right to be heard.

## Communication Strategies

The strategies used to work with agents in a tax law matter will vary, depending on whether you are in the criminal or civil tax division, and at which point during the administrative process you are with respect to either the IRS or a state Department of Taxation. The Ohio Department of Taxation, due to its size in comparison with the IRS, is much less formal to work with, and you can often establish long-standing relationships with various agents within those divisions due to repetitive contact. The IRS on the other hand is a much larger organization; therefore, unless you are assigned to a specific agent, you can find yourself talking with a number of different individuals throughout that system.

I have found that government agents generally prefer written communication supported by backup documentation. The reason for this preferred method of communication is that it provides the agent with the information and backup evidence to prepare a written report for a No Change Letter (a recommendation that there are no changes to the taxpayer's originally filed return), or supports the changes they are proposing as a result of an audit, a request for an appeal, or any other sort of hearing or administrative right that the taxpayer may have.

Technology has not really changed the way I work with tax agencies, as the federal government does not e-mail back and forth with tax attorneys. Their e-mail system currently works only internally. Technology has become helpful, however, in that I am now able to communicate quickly with my clients, and they are able to satisfy information requests very quickly. The client's responses can then be quickly accessed and sent on to the Internal Revenue Service.

## Current Trends in Working with Tax Agencies

I have found that tax agencies tend to be much more cooperative than many people expect; they will generally attempt to be helpful in terms of working to resolve a satisfactory outcome in a client's tax case. However, some of the administrative restructuring that constantly takes place within those agencies tends to be confusing; indeed, the IRS seems to be in a constant state of change with respect to departmentalization in attempting to streamline the very large task of managing millions of tax returns.

With each change in the presidency, there will likely be a change within the Internal Revenue Service in terms of management, and policies and procedures. It is very hard to anticipate what those changes will be without watching and keeping a close eye on legislative activity through various tax publications.

As previously noted, I have found that working with state tax agencies tends to be much less formal than working with the federal government. The IRS has specific procedures, such as its administration appeal process, that one must follow to protect its rights to be heard before the Tax Court and District Court. Although the state agencies also have procedures that must be followed, those procedures tend to be less specific, and their agents tend to work as a collective group to satisfy or resolve a tax problem. When working with the IRS, on the other hand, you tend to be pushed from department to department, depending on what issue you are raising or where you are in an appeal or collection process.

## Common Client Tax Issues

The five most common client tax situations requiring legal assistance are (1) an audit; (2) an appeal of the result of an audit; (3) representation before the tax court; (4) representation with collection matters, including submission of an installment agreement or offer in compromise; and (5) criminal tax prosecution.

Legal tax assistance is generally not required for matters under $25,000; the IRS tends to be flexible with respect to installment payments in those situations. Indeed, the IRS has attempted to provide different areas under which legal assistance is not required, such as an offer and compromise or installment agreement, but my experience has shown that the IRS is much more responsive when a client is represented, as opposed to representing themselves.

## Initial Steps in the Investigation Process

During the initial stages of a tax investigation you will receive an information and document request (IDR) whereby you can begin to surmise what direction the agent is headed with respect to an investigation. In addition, you can simply ask them whether this is a random audit or whether they are looking at issues that were specifically red-flagged on the client's tax return.

If the tax violation turns out to be one of a criminal nature, such as fraud, the investigation will be coming out of the enforcement division of either the IRS or the state Department of Taxation. I typically transfer those cases to an attorney who specializes in the representation of criminal tax clients.

Among the challenges of working with government agents during tax investigations is that you are attempting to satisfy their IDR and provide them with the information that they are requesting without giving them additional information that could take the audit into a different direction such as a position in which the client was aggressive on its interpretation of the code. In other words, you should attempt to keep their focus on the issues that they have addressed in the IDR to the extent that you can. The agent always has the ability to expand the audit, but in most cases, if it has been brought in pursuant to a specific item on the return, they are primarily looking at that particular issue.

### Meeting the Client's Goals

The primary goal and objective when working with government agencies in the area of tax law is to achieve a good result for your client. However, the nature of that result depends on what part of the agency you are dealing with. If you are dealing with an audit, the goal is a No Change Letter or a minimal additional tax exposure. If you are working with a client who is in collections, the goal is to protect the client's assets and to enter into an installment agreement with the IRS or the state Department of Taxation, as the case may be. The objectives are typically identified and developed through conversations with the client.

The strategies that I use to pursue the client's goals are those administrative remedies provided with respect to the IRS and the Ohio Department of Taxation; both agencies provide numerous avenues of appeals with respect to any decision made at any level within the Internal Revenue Service. There are many opportunities to revisit issues and to ultimately reach a solution or outcome that is favorable or acceptable to your client's goals and objectives. At each level, the IRS will attempt to resolve the matter without litigation.

### Preliminary Questions and Information Gathering

The questions that I ask clients in these matters will vary, depending on each individual tax case. The goal is to quickly surmise what the agent is investigating, and then attempt to provide information to satisfy the IDR. It is important to gain an in-depth understanding of your client's position; how the position on their tax return was developed; and what documentation they have to support the position.

The information I obtain and the questions I ask my clients will help develop a strategy as to whether to take a hard stance position with respect to an item that has come into question with respect to a tax return, or to soften the approach. Often there is not a lot of documentation to support a particular deduction, or there are simply holes in the client's position or other existing issues that an agent has overlooked on the return. You will need to consider these issues prior to charging ahead against the IRS and the state Department of Taxation.

I do not have a specific checklist used to prep clients for working with state or federal tax agencies. My general comments are to be prompt with respect to any IDR; be complete and thorough, but do not provide additional information that the agent has not requested; and thirdly, I typically try to have any meetings with the state tax or federal tax agencies at my office or at the office of the accountant who prepared the client's return.

**Overcoming Challenges**

One of the greatest challenges when working with tax agents is that each client believes its case is one of a kind, while the agents have often heard these cases over and over again and therefore sometimes develop a pattern as to their thinking about those individual tax issues.

Fortunately, in some cases we have been able to differentiate our case from the facts under which the agent has pinned them. Typically agents are responsive and open to discussion when you get above the audit level. Field auditors, however, tend to be very focused and fixated on numbers and answers, and do not really want to discuss the legal analysis of any tax issues. To deal with this situation, I move on to the next level.

In most cases the audit process is independent, although most states have compliance statutes that require that if there is a change to a federal tax return, you must report the same to any state agency. Again, the state's procedures tend to be less formal than those of the Internal Revenue Service. Typically, the only cases that involve both the Internal Revenue Service and the state Department of Taxation are employee withholding cases, where the employer has failed to turn over the trust fund portion of the employee's withholdings to the IRS and the state in which it is operating. In those cases, you will need to work with both agencies at the same time in order to come up with a resolution for getting those funds made whole.

One of the unique challenges of working with the Internal Revenue Service is the multiple avenues upon which you can pursue an appeal of a tax issue, or question a lien or levy action. Keeping up with the administrative changes within the Internal Revenue Service is probably the largest challenge, as the number of persons to which you should report or speak with changes periodically.

## The Role of the Client

Most clients typically have little or no experience with tax agency interaction. Therefore, I generally try to keep the client in the background as much as possible when facilitating a relationship with a tax agency. If I need their assistance or their participation at a meeting because they have information that can help our position, I will have them present. Otherwise, I typically tend to meet with an agent without the client being present.

The client's responsibility in working with tax agents is to be honest, forthright, and provide the information that they have. If a client attempts to protect a lie or an incorrect position that they knowingly took on a return, and continues to deceive the IRS or any state tax agency, that strategy will ultimately backfire against them.

## Providing Documentation: Helpful Resources

The timeline of working with a government agency on a tax matter will vary, based on both the agency itself and the accurateness and thoroughness with which the client can respond to the information/document request. If the agent is forced to make request after request in order to get a clear understanding of the case, the case will typically take much longer and be dragged out. Conversely, if the client has clean files and is able to access and provide information that is readily understandable by the agency involved, the tax situation is most likely to be resolved rather quickly.

The documents that are gathered and generated when working with the IRS will depend on what has been requested. Typically, the client will prepare any exhibits related to the documents, or the actual document upon which we are relying. The attorney involved is typically responsible for drafting a response based on the client's knowledge and the documents provided.

Both the state of Ohio and the Internal Revenue Service have their own Web sites which provide a substantial amount of procedural information. The disadvantages of using these resources is that they tend to produce information, news releases, or press releases that tend to favor the government's position; therefore, you have to be cautious about the information that you are gathering from either of those Web sites.

## Potential Outcomes

The potential outcomes for each client's tax situation will vary, depending on the department with which you are involved. The tax situations that have the most severe consequences are those where the client has failed to report income or has taken the trust fund portion of an employee's withholding tax. Both of these situations are viewed very seriously by the Internal Revenue Service and can result in jail time. Clients who do not file their income tax returns face criminal prosecution by the Internal Revenue Service.

Client expectations tend to be high with respect to outcomes before the Internal Revenue Service. In most cases, they feel that they are entitled to the deductions or the treatment of a tax position that they have taken, and do not understand why the IRS would differ in that position.

If you are dealing with an audit, the outcome is that you will have either proposed changes to the tax return, or you will receive a No Change Letter from the auditing agent. You must then work your way though the appeals process, hoping to reverse the decision of the auditing agents by filing a tax protest (federal) or petition for reassessment (Ohio). Outcomes in the collection process will vary based on each client's income and financial capabilities to satisfy the assessed amount.

## Preventative Efforts

The preventative efforts that I recommend to clients will also vary based on each individual situation. In some instances, I will ultimately recommend that the client discontinue their business operations if they are failing to meet their tax withholding obligations, because they will only make a bad situation worse if their liability continues to grow, and personal responsibility attaches to them in their individual capacity.

In a general audit situation, I advise clients to keep strong records and files with respect to the deductions that they are taking on their returns. They should keep copies of all receipts of their payables and have supporting documentation to back up any of the positions that they have taken on their tax return, whether it be a deduction, a position on income, or otherwise.

## Final Thoughts

The most important piece of advice that I can offer any client who is facing a tax investigation is to get a tax attorney involved at the time of the initial contact with the tax agency you are working with. Getting an attorney involved early on does two things. First, the presence of an attorney at the initial meeting does not alert the tax agent to there being a potential problem. If, however, an attorney or an accountant begins to get involved in the representation partway through the process, it can sometimes raise an eyebrow or throw a red flag to the auditing agent. Secondly, it is never a good idea to attempt to go through this process alone—in most cases, if you do not have legal representation, you will have a negative result.

The key to achieving success in any representation involving a tax agency is to have factual documents to support the position you have taken, and to be honest and forthright with the tax agency involved. In most cases, following that strategy will help you to achieve a successful and reasonable outcome with respect to your tax matter.

*Scot C. Crow, a partner for Roetzel & Andress, focuses his practice in matters involving private wealth management, business succession planning and exit strategies, general taxation, design and implementation of non-qualified deferred compensation plans, civil representation of tax matters before the Ohio Department of Taxation and Internal Revenue Service, and asset protection planning. He also handles probate estate administration and trust administration. Mr. Crow's clients consist primarily of closely held businesses and their owners, high net worth individuals and families, corporate executives, and nonprofit public and private foundations.*

*Mr. Crow is a member of the Columbus Bar Association, the Ohio State Bar Association, the Columbus Estate Planning Council Group II, the Ohio Manufacturing Association's Tax Policy Committee, and the Financial Planning Association.*

*Mr. Crow was selected as an "Ohio Super Lawyers - Rising Star" by* Law & Politics *magazine and* Cincinnati Magazine *(2005, 2006, 2007). He is a Certified Financial Planner*™ *and certified as a financial expert witness for the U.S. District Court and Southern District of Ohio. He is a licensed Ohio Life and Health Insurance Agent. Mr. Crow is the co-author of :Estate Planning Essentials: Protecting Your Family and Your Legacy,"* The Smarter Physician, *2007, and* Sixth Circuit Declares Ohio's Manufacturing Tax Credit Unconstitutional.

*Mr. Crow received his J.D. from Capital University, Law School, Order of the Curie, his LL.M. from Capital University, Taxation, Order of the Curie, and his B.S. from Franciscan University.*

# Defending Clients' State and Local Tax Issues

Joseph C. Bright

*Partner*

WolfBlock LLP

ASPATORE

As a tax attorney, I handle just about everything that has to do with state and local taxes—i.e., tax planning; transaction analysis; audits; appeals; regulatory work, including trying to get regulations adopted or changed; and legislative work, trying to get legislation adopted or changed. A major focus is state and local tax litigation.

I aim to offer value to clients in several ways. First, by concentrating heavily on state and local taxation, I have broad and deep exposure and experience across a large number of tax areas, including income taxes; sales tax; transfer taxes; vehicle tax; utility taxes; financial institution taxes; real property tax; and gross receipts taxes. Each of these tax areas is nominally a discrete area. Yet, many issues crop up in more than one tax area, such as: is there nexus (a taxable connection), is the tax basis calculated correctly, and is an apportion amount required. The more you know about these common themes, the more useful information you can bring to bear on any particular client problem.

Additionally, I have gained an appreciation of how governments look at tax issues. I once served as chief counsel for the Pennsylvania Department of Revenue. That position gave me a useful perspective on how the government looks at many tax problems. About four years ago, I was appointed to the Pennsylvania Business Tax Reform Commission and charged by the governor to examine all business taxation in Pennsylvania and make recommendations for improvement. That assignment gave me a useful, independent perspective on tax issues. In addition, I believe that my longtime involvement in state and local tax litigation gives me a valuable perspective on what is actually likely to happen to a client in a particular situation.

**Current Trends in Tax Law**

A major trend in state and local tax law is a combination of two key concepts: one is the degree to which a particular state will try to combine business entities—treat them as one taxpayer—or break down the separate identity of taxpayers by disallowing the effects of transactions between them. The second concept is the exploration of what a taxpayer can do by way of structural planning to reduce its tax burden. These concepts work in opposition; governments often try to break down the barriers between separate entities, and businesses try to take advantage of them. Pennsylvania is a bit unusual in that historically, and still to date, it is a strictly separate company state; we do not have unitary taxation, consolidated reporting, or expense disallowance. Expense disallowance can undo in whole or in part tax advantages that depend on separate company reporting. On occasion, the Department of Revenue has tried to accomplish the equivalent of expense disallowance, but not with much success, and in any event nowhere near to the extent that some other states have done. A related issue is the concept of nexus—what acts within a state justify imposition of a tax burden. The decision that returns are not required in a particular state can affect many tax years because generally no statute of limitations applies if no returns are filed. The Financial Accounting Standards Board Interpretation No. 48 recently put the problem into greater focus, because for public companies it requires analysis and quantification of income tax positions taken by the company.

Our firm deals with clients in other states. Even if we are looking just at a Pennsylvania issue, it is useful to know how similar issues are treated in other states. Business structuring and restructuring is one of the major topics we deal with, and while it primarily affects income taxation, it might also affect other forms of business taxation such as net worth or transfer taxes. It is important to help clients to understand the degree to which a business structure can be used to tax advantage, and the degree to which the government can stop you from doing so.

Another area where I see a lot of activity—particularly in Pennsylvania, although also in other states—is real estate and real property taxation. The real property tax is frequently criticized as being regressive; there have been many calls for its reduction or abolition, but there is little consensus over what, if anything, should replace it. Property values may continue to drop in the coming months, but then they will go back up; in any case, this will continue to be an area of increased attention.

## Unique Challenges of Pennsylvania Tax Law

Even though Pennsylvania is a separate company taxing state, and even though officials have repeatedly said that they are not going to try to force unitary taxation or assume disallowance powers that they do not have, they nonetheless look closely at business structures that have the effect, in their view, of artificially reducing the tax base. In many cases you can successfully deal with these examinations; sometimes you cannot. This continues to be a challenge for clients and their attorneys.

We are seeing an increased proliferation of pass-through entities in this state, i.e., S corporations, partnerships, LLCs—entities that for federal and many other tax purposes are not treated as taxpayers. Recently, Pennsylvania formed a pass-through business unit in the Department of Revenue that is charged with looking at these entities' returns to see whether income is being correctly reported. Although Pennsylvania's Personal Income Tax rate is low at 3.07 percent, nonetheless it is a gross receipts tax, not a net income tax, so there can be a lot of money involved in transactions that take place in entities. The new focus in this area has created a lot of work and problems for taxpayers.

## The Role of Global Competition on State and Federal Tax Issues

A major political factor affecting state and federal tax issues is global competition. Repeated studies show that corporations in the U.S. are overtaxed compared to their competitors. If a U.S. company is competing with a Chinese company, the Chinese company may already have a real advantage in terms of the cost of labor, but there may also be a substantial differential in the tax burden. The greater the tax burden on a U.S. company, the more difficult it is to compete—and the more pressure there is on the business to reduce its taxes as much as possible. Simply put, since U.S. businesses feel that they are being overtaxed compared to others, they are going to put pressure on their staff to try legitimately to reduce that burden. The CEO will ask the tax director, Why is our effective tax rate out of line with our competitors? This trend drives many of the tax reduction ideas for business restructuring strategies. States will accuse a business of going too far in an effort to reduce its taxes—they may claim that a certain restructuring lacks substance, or is a sham. While any restructuring transaction must be done lawfully, we should remember that businesses typically are responding to a real economic need when they attempt to reduce their tax burden by structuring. A particular business cannot do much about the impact of global competition. Probably the best a business can do is to try to take advantage of structuring opportunities that will be respected, if used correctly, in order to cut the tax costs of the business. While businesses acting together can get taxes reduced if the group is determined and can make a good case, relief from such an effort is speculative and rarely immediate.

**Preliminary Client Meetings: Key Questions and Research**

When first meeting with a client about a state or local tax issue, it is critical to look carefully at the specific type of problem the business has—i.e., is the state taxing beyond its borders? Is the government taking too much of the business's economic pie? Is the government trying to attack a structure the client has set up? Can the business keep using it, and what are the chances of success if they do? Is the government asserting a tax that the client thinks they are not entitled to? Is the taxpayer entitled to a refund? It is especially important to understand the procedural context of the taxpayer's issue. For example, is the client currently involved in a transaction, and if so, when do they want to close it? Is the client involved in an assessment, and if so, when does the appeal or refund period expire. In Pennsylvania, that date is critical, because it ends the period during which you can appeal or petition for a refund.

Once you understand what the government is doing and what the taxpayer is doing in relation to a certain issue, and you understand the time deadlines that are involved, then you need to figure out the legal principles that come into play—in particular, the statutes, regulations, or case law that will come to bear on the client's particular issue. It is essential quickly and surgically to cut through to what those key legal principles are. While there are usually a number of legal principles involved in a tax case, a few or perhaps only one will be critical; the rest are sidelights. In many cases there will be some resources such as treatises, thoughtful articles, and particularly good judicial opinions that you can consult to help you get your arms around these issues.

Simply put, during these preliminary stages you need to perform a process of triage, segregating the elements of the collision between the taxpayer and the government, and then correctly assess what key principles will govern the case, and how they are likely to be applied. It could be that the client understands what the current law is, but they want to get it changed, and they want to know how they can mount an effort to do that—but there is quite a difference between developing a battle plan for dealing with a specific assessment dispute, as opposed to assessing the possibility of getting a regulation or statute changed. Dealing with an assessment issue is more focused—you need to evaluate what the government is assessing and what the appeal period is, and then you can hone in on how good the government's case is. Getting a regulation or statute changed is a much more complicated process, and invites considering what is the optimum result for the client given how interested parties are likely to line up on the issue.

## Key Legal Skills for a Tax or Audit Appeal

I believe that the most important legal skill that is needed to handle client tax or audit appeals is the ability to perform the kind of analysis that will quickly and correctly determine the key legal principles in the case, be they statutory, regulatory, or case law. You need to know what matters and what does not matter, and why. Experience can help you to reach the right conclusions, but a good tax lawyer will always work analytically to focus quickly and efficiently on what matters in the client's situation. Analytic ability is difficult to create; to some extent, you either have it or you do not. It can be improved upon, but if you do not have an aptitude for analytic thinking then you probably should not be doing tax law. If you do have an aptitude for analysis, then the question is how do you make it better—i.e., how do you become quicker and more efficient at taking apart a problem to determine its constituent pieces. For example, if a business is entitled to apportionment and none is provided by statute, then what? What is the order of the court likely to say?

Another critical legal skill is the ability to communicate to the client, to tell the client succinctly and accurately what key principles are going to come to bear on their problem and what the likely result will be. You must also be able to communicate effectively with the government if you want to convince them that their case is not good, is only fair, misses the point, or is correct but has gone too far.

## Best Practices and Strategies for Dealing with Tax Law Issues

The most effective tax strategies for a client will depend on the issues in which they are involved. For example, a client may tell us, "We had a huge transaction and realized a big gain, but we didn't realize it in Pennsylvania; we realized it in another state. Therefore, Pennsylvania has no business trying to take a piece of that gain." There is a whole set of doctrines that deal with that type of issue, including those pertaining to non-business income, and operational vs. investment income as explained in *Allied-Signal Inc. v. Director, Division of Taxation,* 504 U.S. 768 (1992) and *MeadWestvaco Corp. v. Illinois Department of Revenue,* _553__ U.S. ____ (2008). In Pennsylvania, we also have the doctrines of unrelated assets and multiformity, which are analogous to the *Allied Signal* doctrine. These are some of the tools to use to try to avoid having Pennsylvania take a piece of a transaction, which the client thinks they should not tax at all.

The use of these strategies assumes that the client has come to you after the fact; however, if the client is coming to you for advice with respect to a future transaction, you have a lot more leeway in terms of strategies; you can explain to the client that structuring the transaction in a certain way will give them a better chance of reducing their tax burden. Whether you are looking at a transaction that has already happened, or one that is going to happen (in which case you have the opportunity to structure it ahead of time), the strategy in both cases is to first get a solid grip on the facts in light of what the client wants to do. You need to know exactly how their business is set up; what their transactions are like; what they are selling; how they make their money; and what they do in other states. Next, you need to figure out what the relevant principles are, and how you can apply them to this particular situation. You cannot simply go through a twenty-statute checklist, because there are a number of statutes that will have no bearing on the client's case. Rather, it is important to assess the situation first then use your experience and judgment based on other situations to figure out what the key pieces of the case are.

## Red Flags and Monitoring Client Compliance

The tax violations that are probably most likely to result in an agency investigation in the income and sales tax areas is unremitted tax that a business has collected from other people. For example, if you have collected sales tax that has not been turned over to the government, it is a serious problem that can turn into a criminal violation in a particularly bad case. Another red flag in the business context that may lead to an investigation is any difference between federal and state reporting, or federal or state reporting that differs from what appears in a press or an annual report. There are many apportionment, exclusion, and transaction issues to be aware of; the government will be looking for any violations in those areas, and if they see them, they will ask about them.

Therefore, in order to handle a client's tax dispute or issue properly, it is important to monitor client compliance with all applicable laws and statues carefully. First and foremost, all documentation in relation to the issue is critical; if the client has had contacts with the government it is important to write them down, keep a running count, and always be responsive—even if being responsive means saying, "We don't have that information yet," or "We are trying to get it," or "We don't think you are entitled to it." Communication with the government, and careful documentation of exactly who said what, is essential.

Quantification of these issues is important too. If the client is concerned about state sales taxes, it is important to monitor how many sales have taken place, and over what period of time. It is also important to consider how the client has compiled that data, and how much confidence they have in the data—does it reflect what is really going on? Documentation of all communications and business transactions with respect to the client's particular problem—and ongoing communication with the government with respect to that issue—is of key importance.

**Key State and Local Agencies in Tax Law Issues**

The key state and local agencies that are responsible for developing, investigating, and enforcing tax laws will vary by state; in Pennsylvania, the key agency is the Department of Revenue, but it can also be the Office of the Attorney General, if the client has already been assessed or the matter is in collection mode. The Department of Revenue examines returns; conducts audits of taxpayers; and issues assessments. If an appeal is filed, lawyers from the Attorney General's Office will become involved, although it is still the Department of Revenue's case.

At the local level, the key regulatory agency largely depends on the jurisdiction that is conducting the investigation. In Philadelphia, there is a Department of Revenue similar to the Pennsylvania Department of Revenue, and in other localities, an outside contractor may act as a tax collector.

The role of these agencies is primarily focused on investigation and assessment; a tax audit is not like civil litigation where the plaintiff files a complaint and must prove a case. The government holds powerful cards, generally speaking, beginning with broad powers of investigation. Government tax officials can look at all kinds of things, and they rarely have to justify to anybody what they want to investigate. Furthermore, when they make an assessment or take an action they are presumably correct, quite unlike typical civil litigation. Essentially, the plaintiff in these matters does not have to prove a case—if the department says that you owe $150,000, that is presumptively correct, and the burden switches to you to disprove it. Thus, the government comes armed in these cases with powerful tools that people do not have in other legal contexts.

## Key Steps In Working with Government Agencies on an Audit Issue

The first objective in any tax dispute situation is to try to get the government to focus on what they really want from the client. Audit letters often contain a long laundry list of issues that need to be looked at, although in most cases the government actually only may be interested in a few of those issues. Therefore, it is important to contact the official you are dealing with and ask, "What is it that you really want?" If they are reluctant to circumscribe their own audit, you can ask them what issue they want to start with, which at least provides the advantage of focusing the inquiry. In many cases, the government may never get to the other items they originally cited, because they did not really need to know about them.

Therefore, it is always important to find out what the government is really interested in, and then respond in a reasonably timely and comprehensive way. If the government thinks that you are not cooperating, they have powerful tools to make you cooperate, and it can cause them to look with suspicion on issues that they might not otherwise look at all. It is important to build trust and confidence with the government officials, so that they believe that you are going to respond to what they care about.

As part of this process, you must get yourself and your client focused on what legal principles are going to bear on those areas that the government is interested in, and what facts you are going to have to come up with in order to convince them that you are correct. Basically, you must try to focus the inquiry to the extent that you can, and then you must get your client focused on what the key issues are. Of course, those key issues may change. You may start out by focusing on Issue 1, and be able to satisfy the government in that area, and they may then decide that they want to look at Issue 2. However, I believe that if you approach the process in a focused way you have a greater chance of making a coherent and useful response to whatever it is the government is after.

During this process, you need to assemble the facts and the data in relation to the case—all transactions and descriptions of activity—and dig in as deeply as you can. Frequently, your client's tax people are not operational people; they have information that is given to them by others in the company. Sometimes the information is good; sometimes it is not. You may ask the tax director a question, and if he gets his information from people in the field you do not always know if it is correct. Therefore, you often have to push for more information within the company, because you do not want to go out on a limb with respect to a certain claim, only to find out that the facts do not support it. You must help your client get the facts that they need to support their case, although their operational people may resist this process; there can be a tendency to give short shrift to an investigation that someone else in the business is handling. Operations and sales people do not see tax audits as contributing to the sales of goods and services. That, of course, is shortsighted.

Throughout this process, it is important to communicate properly with the government. If you cannot meet a deadline, go to the official in advance and tell them that you are having problems. Most government auditors are much more likely to go along with you if you are constantly responsive, and if they do not get the feeling that you have ignored them, or think that over time they will lose interest and go away.

Once you see that the government is reaching a position with respect to your client's case, you need to explore whether they are open to other considerations, and try to get them to accept a different position in relation to your client's case. It is important to do this before the government issues its final assessment, whereupon your only recourse is the appellate process.

## Overcoming Challenges in Dealing with Tax Issues

The biggest challenge that is involved in dealing with government agencies that are investigating a client's tax issues is getting everybody involved—the government, the lawyer, and the client—and focused on the issues that really count. The second key challenge is pulling together the applicable law, and the facts that bear on that law. Quite frequently you will not have all of the facts that you need, although it would be best if you had a detailed account of exactly what everybody did in relation to the issue.

It is important to put yourself in the position of the government with respect to what it is that they are really looking for, and if you do not have exactly what they want in terms of information, you need to find out if there is some other way that you can satisfy them that your view of the transaction is correct. In many cases, you can work with the government to see if you can arrive at a practical resolution of the facts necessary to deal with the situation. For example, if the client only has 80 percent of the necessary sales tax records, you need to figure out a way to extrapolate what the missing records contain based on other extrinsic evidence, and then get the government to accept that as a reasonable solution.

It is always of the utmost importance to try to understand an audit from the auditors' point of view. You have to understand what they are doing and why; what their charge is; what they are concerned about; and what they are not concerned about. Sometimes you are not going to satisfy them, but in many cases you can deal with certain issues and even make them go away, simply by not fighting the auditor on every single issue. You have to figure out what it is they really want to know, and if there is something that you can show them that will deal with the concern that they have.

Similarly, you need to find out what upsets your client the most about the government's charges in this audit transaction. Just because the client is annoyed does not mean that you can automatically obtain the relief they are seeking, but if you understand their point of view, your chances of addressing the issue successfully are increased.

## Final Thoughts

In summary, I believe that there are three key factors to getting through these problems successfully: focus, communication, and responsiveness. You need to be focused on what really counts; you need to communicate effectively with the government and your client so that it is clear what everybody is supposed to be doing; and you need to be responsive so that the government understands that you hear what they are saying, and that you are trying to do something about it in a timely manner. Keeping those three factors in mind will maximize the chance that your client's audit will stay focused and civilized.

*Joseph C. Bright is a partner in WolfBlock's Tax Practice Group, where he concentrates in state and local taxation.*

*A former chief counsel of the Pennsylvania Department of Revenue (1980 81), Mr. Bright has since represented hundreds of taxpayers in state and local tax planning, administrative, legislative, and litigation matters.*

*Mr. Bright is the author of* Taxation, *a two-volume treatise on Pennsylvania state and local taxation published by West Group as part of* Summary of Pennsylvania Jurisprudence 2d. *A book review of* Taxation *in* State Tax Notes *described the first edition of the treatise as the leading treatise on Pennsylvania state taxation and Mr. Bright as one of the leading state practitioners in the nation. He is a principal Pennsylvania correspondent for* State Tax Notes, *published by Tax Analysts, Inc. He has written hundreds of articles on state and local tax topics. Mr. Bright was appointed by the leadership of the House of Representatives to the Pennsylvania Business Tax Reform Commission. He is a Fellow of the American College of Tax Counsel and is listed in* Who's Who in America.

*Mr. Bright is an active member of the Tax Section of the Pennsylvania Bar Association, the State and Local Tax Committee of the Tax Section of the Philadelphia Bar Association, the Tax Section of the American Bar Association, the Tax Committee of the Pennsylvania Chamber of Business and Industry, and the State and Local Tax Committee of the Greater Philadelphia Chamber of Business and Industry. In local civic affairs, Mr. Bright is a board member of the Economy League of Greater Philadelphia. He has served as vice-chair of the Children's Hospital Foundation and member of the Board of Managers, president of the Board of Trustees of St. Peter's School in Philadelphia, president of the Society Hill Civic Association, and Trustee of the Philadelphia General Hospital Research Fund.*

*Mr. Bright received his B.A., cum laude, from Harvard University in 1964, and his J.D., cum laude, from the University of Pennsylvania Law School in 1970, where he was the managing editor of the* University of Pennsylvania Law Review. *He also served as a lieutenant in the United States Army from 1965 to 1967, receiving a Bronze Star Medal for Meritorious Service..*

# Mississippi State and Local Tax Law Issues for Client Companies


Louis G. Fuller

*Member*

Brunini, Grantham, Grower & Hewes PLLC



ASPATORE

The primary focus of my practice is assisting clients with Mississippi franchise, income, and sales and use tax matters; I also assist new and expanding business in taking advantage of state and local incentives designed to attract such businesses and industrial development to this state. In addition to some local clients in the sales and use tax area, I have a large multistate client practice where I am able to offer my clients the benefit of my very specific expertise in Mississippi state tax law. Since Mississippi does not have a great deal of published law, perhaps the greatest value I can provide to clients is knowledge I have gained through my years of experience working with the Mississippi State Tax Commission, referred to herein as the "Commission."

## Trouble Spots to Avoid

*Be Attentive to the Specifics of Mississippi Law*

Mississippi is a small state and a client's Mississippi tax liability general represents a relatively small part of a company's total state and local tax liability. Understandably, the Mississippi return or the impact of Mississippi law on tax planning may not get as much attention as the laws of other states in which the client may do business. Like many states, Mississippi has begun to frown on what it perceives to be improper tax planning or shifting of income and its examiners can be aggressive when they uncover filing positions that they do not believe are well founded. In tight budget times, Mississippi is protective of its tax base. For these reasons, Mississippi has taken several steps to protect its fisc and to curb perceived abuses. For example, Mississippi was one of the first states to enact royalty add-back provisions to combat intangibles holding companies. Mississippi does not allow deductions for interest on indebtedness incurred to pay dividends. Mississippi has also enacted substantial penalty provisions for "fraudulent" returns and their definition of fraud can be broad. These can be traps for the unwary.

*Cooperation with Examiners*

I will also talk about this later, but in almost every significant tax matter I handle I receive reports either from the client or from the Commission that the audit experience was unpleasant, if not combative. I recognize that such an approach can be a strategy, but many times, I find that the conflict was due to alleged lack of responsiveness on the part of the client to the requests of the auditors. I suspect other practitioners' experiences are the same. Frequently, resolving the hard feelings that carry over from that experience paves the way for settlement on appeal. I often wonder whether the proposed assessments would have been smaller and penalty assessments less likely if such disputes were resolved earlier or avoided altogether.

## Tax Law Enforcement

For most state taxes, the primary enforcement agency is the Commission. For property taxes, enforcement is the combined responsibility of the Commission and local city and county tax assessors and collectors. The state's attorney general does not play a significant role in tax enforcement action, but in the property tax area, the Attorney General's office will provide guidance to local tax assessors and collectors in the form of opinions interpreting state law. With respect to incentives, the Mississippi Development Authority plays an important role in administering many of the state's tax incentive programs. This role includes certifying enterprises as eligible for the particular incentives, negotiating or approving fees in lieu of tax agreements.

## Working with State Tax Investigators and Enforcers

In terms of enforcement, I work mostly with the Commission representing taxpayers in examinations and appeals. Many of these clients already have sophisticated tax departments in charge of compliance and examination, and if they do not, they often have outside CPAs who are doing their tax returns and can deal with the examination process. Such clients may not engage a lawyer until the matter has reached the end stages of an audit, at which time there may be one or two important legal issues that need to be dealt with such as a fair apportionment calculation or the classification of an item of income as business or non-business income. In fact, Mississippi does not require a lawyer to handle an appeal; its appeal processes are fairly informal, and a taxpayer can even appeal a case on their own. However, I believe that in many cases I can do the most good in the early stages of an examination or appeal, especially if the client wishes to resolve the issue at the earliest possible point in time. As my practice has matured, I often find that my knowledge of the Commission's informal policies or how the Commission has dealt with a similar issue in the past can really help.

The Mississippi State Tax Commission administers the state's tax laws; therefore it really has two functions—it has an administrative side that handles policies and rule making, and it has an enforcement side that covers examinations and audits. Our role as tax attorneys involves working with both sides of the Commission. For example, we frequently work with clients who are contemplating a significant transaction in Mississippi. In these cases, we will meet in advance with the top administrative officials of the Commission and request a private letter ruling or obtain informal advice on how the Commission would interpret and apply the applicable law. Audits and appeals are more adversarial and our charge is to protect the client's interests to ensure a fair and appropriate result.

## Key Issues When Working with Government Agents

### *Audits and Appeals*

When I take on a new tax matter, the first thing I will do is gather all of the relevant facts. If I am entering the case at a later stage, I want to know everything that has gone before and I want to see all correspondence that has passed between the taxpayer and the Commission. I need to know everything that the client has told the Commission and everything the Commission has told the client. I then need to determine what the client perceives to be the key issues and the client's position with respect to those issues; I will also ask the client what it believes the Commission's position is on those same issues, to the extent that can be known. Unfortunately, you often do not know the Commission's position or why an adjustment was made until later in the process. In many cases, I have seen similar adjustments and can provide some insight. This is sometimes an area where I can be of significant help to the client. In other cases, you just have to ask the Commission and I generally know how to get to that information.

We then identify the appropriate body of law, or specific points of law we are dealing with, and develop our argument.

Each circumstance is different. Some are very fact intensive like multistate apportionment issues, which may require significant analysis to determine the appropriate status of sales. In other cases, there is no factual dispute so the case turns strictly upon a proper interpretation of law. An example may be whether particular income is business or non-business income. Consequently, different facts and issues will dictate the course of your preparation in a tax law matter.

## Tax Law Challenges

One of the most common challenges in Mississippi tax practice can be finding sufficient state law or authority to guide you in your decisions. Unlike many other states, Mississippi does not publish orders of its administrative appeals bodies or private letter rulings. Additionally, Chancery Court decisions, the first level of judicial appeal, are not published and there are few reported Appeals and Supreme Court cases. Therefore, we do not have a large body of case law available for public consumption. Consequently, it is not uncommon for there to be a real question as to how the law should be applied in a particular case. In the context of examinations, it may be difficult to understand the position an auditor is taking on a particular issue. This is where there is no substitute for experience. Frequently, a client will describe an adjustment that just doesn't make sense to them, but I may immediately recognize it as a very common issue raised on an exam. In such a case, I can often enlighten the client by explaining the state's usual position in such a situation and whether the auditor's proposals are consistent with past precedent or policy.

## Primary Goals and Objectives When Working with Government Agencies

I always want to know what the client wants to accomplish in relation to their tax matter—the goal we are working to achieve—and we will then plot out the strategy to best accomplish that goal. For example, in some situations a client company is trying to decide whether to locate a plant or other facility in Mississippi. In most cases, companies have already narrowed their choice of location to just a few states. In such cases, we work with the client and the state to determine the best match of incentives with the project. In many cases, our client and the state are working toward a common objective—i.e., the location of the plant in Mississippi. Therefore, we will work with the state in a joint effort to assemble an incentives package that will make locating here a good economic choice for the client at a reasonable economic cost to the state.

In more adversarial situations, I always want to know what is important and significant to the client, and what may be part of a larger strategy. For example, I want to know if the client has the same issue in several states, or if it is important that we set a precedent in this matter—or not. Is this issue something that they are willing to resolve early on by reaching a compromise, or is it significant enough that the client is willing to defend the assessment aggressively? For example, there are some issues on which a multistate client can be whipsawed if two states take different positions with respect to the company's income, such as gain on the sale of a division or subsidiary.

In recent years the importance of financial accounting reserves for the payment of taxes has become an increasingly significant issue for many companies—if a company does not have sufficient reserves and a tax issue comes up, it can have serious financial statement implications for them. Disclosure issues have also become increasingly important, as more companies have come under scrutiny with respect to their tax liabilities. Indeed, a number of recent rule changes are requiring public companies to be more forthcoming in their tax disclosures, and to apply sharper pencils to their tax reserves and allowances. Consequently, state tax issues are of a greater importance from a financial standpoint for many public companies these days.

## Recent Trends in Working with Tax Agencies

Mississippi has an appointed State Tax Commission consisting of three commissioners who serve rotating six-year terms. The chairman sets the tone and direction for the agency. Our current chairman is an attorney, and he has been more sensitive to taxpayer appeals and controversies than the Commission has been in the past. During his tenure our administrative appeals statutes have been amended to afford greater rights to taxpayers and to roll back the standard of review in judicial appeals. The Commission has also adopted new administrative rules governing appeals and taxpayer rights.

The State Tax Commission's central operations are housed in a single building located in a suburb of the state capital. Recently though, the chairman has moved the body of taxpayer appeals to a building in the Capitol complex affording the taxpayer some sense of an independent appeals process. Taxpayers need to feel they are going to receive an independent and fair review of their case, and our current chairman seems more sensitive to that.

There is always an ebb and flow in this area; it appears there are periods when the Commission is more or less aggressive in its audit and compliance efforts and audit activity increases and decreases accordingly. However, while the Tax Commission may be more or less active in different areas from time to time, it is safe to say they are always going to be looking at large multistate taxpayers. Mississippi does not have much industry or corporations headquartered within the state, and tax administrators and lawmakers have perceived historically that our state has been on the short end of a lot of multistate tax planning. Consequently, the Commission is very sensitive to efforts to "shift income" out of the state and Mississippi has been at the forefront of adopting laws and audit strategies to combat common multistate tax planning strategies. For example, Mississippi was one of the first states to adopt the intangibles add-back statutes for royalties paid to intangibles holding companies, which many large multistate companies use to reduce their overall state tax burden. We also have a statute designed to disallow interest on debt incurred to pay dividends to combat a common strategy used by many multistate companies to convert non-deductible dividends to deductible interest, and thus reduce its overall state tax burden.

Since Mississippi is so aggressive in combating many common tax planning techniques, one of my challenges when I have a multistate client pertains to the fact they may not be aware of some of these state policies—and unless I alert them to these issues, they can run into problems.

## Client Tax Situations Requiring Legal Assistance

Creating incentives for industrial development is an area where legal assistance is commonly necessary, and I use the term "industrial" loosely because Mississippi is currently offering incentives for a variety of projects. For example, we offer incentives to attract high-tech businesses, not just manufacturing companies. These include incentives for research and development enterprises, data and information processing enterprises, and motion picture companies. Mississippi also offers enhanced incentives for projects representing large capital investment and significant new employment. Examples of such "major economic impact" projects include the Nissan plant that broke ground in 2000 and the Toyota project that will be completed in 2010. Consequently, there is often an opportunity to tailor the incentives our state offers to a particular client company.

The second area that tax lawyers commonly work in is tax examinations and appeals. Most of my clients have internal tax departments that are familiar with the details in this area, but if a particularly large issue arises at examination, outside legal assistance may be required—and we will certainly be called in during the appeals process.

We are also frequently called in as state tax counsel for large M&A transactions that are taking place in our state. We are consulted on the tax implications of a particular transaction—i.e., are there going to be sales taxes? What are the income tax implications? What is the best type of entity to use in order to acquire and hold these assets?

Voluntary disclosure is another area where clients typically need legal assistance—the client may discover that they should have been filing returns, or they may find that they have not been collecting a certain tax that they should have been collecting. Such cases often involve questions of nexus; that is, whether the company's level of activity within Mississippi has risen to the point that there is significant connection to the state to justify the imposition of a state tax. While Mississippi does not have a formal voluntary disclosure program, they do accept such inquiries and generally work with the client to minimize the potential taxes and liability depending upon the particular circumstances involved.

In many cases there is also lawyer involvement in the property tax area. The annual rendering, assessment, and protest process is very prescribed by statute and generally strictly construed. Property tax incentives generally require the assistance of lawyers. For example, any project with capital investment exceeding $100 million is entitled to enter into a fee-in-lieu of taxes agreement with the local authorities, subject to the approval of the MDA.

As previously stated, legal assistance is generally not required at the earliest levels of tax examinations and appeals; CPAs and client tax departments typically handle the process at that stage. Lawyers may not be involved in the process unless there arises a particularly difficult legal issue, or until the matter reaches appeals. Occasionally I am engaged to assist in the background for a strategic reason; that is, out of concern that if lawyers get involved in a tax matter early on, it may send a signal to enforcers that the stakes are high for the client. In such circumstances, I often consult with regional or national firms that are actually handling an audit, and I simply assist them with the procedural requirements.

## Working Effectively with Tax Agency Investigators

Although I do not use formal checklists, the process of preparing clients for working with state agencies on a tax matter is not unlike a federal tax audit situation. First and foremost, you need to be truthful, and you need to be responsive to all inquiries. Different clients have different sensibilities in this regard; some are simply less forthcoming than others are. An old adage that holds true in these situations is to always answer the question that is being asked, but only that question—do not answer questions that have not been asked, because you need to remember that you are in an adversarial circumstance in an examination.

It is also important to keep in mind that there are sensitivities to be aware of in state tax issues, because the various state tax authorities communicate with each other; therefore, in some cases the implications of a client's tax matter extend beyond the borders of one particular state. In addition, if there are ongoing cases in other states, the taxpayer cannot take a position in one state that differs from the position they are taking in another state.

Essentially, it is important that the client be forthcoming; indeed, auditors often complain that they have asked the client for a certain piece of information on numerous occasions without a response. Many of these issues can be resolved by being responsive and providing information on a timely basis. At the same time it is important to be alert to relevance—if you recognize that something is just a fishing expedition, state your objections and take it to the auditor's supervisor if necessary. If, however, the agency is asking for information they are entitled to get, you should give it to them in a timely and complete fashion, as that raises the level of cooperation in an investigation and gets things moving. Clients need to understand that because auditors are on the other side of what is a potentially contentious situation, they are trained to be suspicious and ask many questions—it is not their job to just accept what you have told them at face value. They are going to look behind your words.

**Successful Strategies for Dealing with Tax Audits**

Most of the companies that I deal with have tax departments with certain protocols in place with respect to how to deal with tax auditors; for example, they may have one person assigned to work with the auditor and get him or her the information requested. It is important to ask the auditor to put all requests in writing. This is in both your and the auditor's interest.

If the client does not have clear protocols on how to deal with a tax examination and a CPA has been filing their tax returns, I will recommend that the audit be conducted at the CPA's office. It is important to have tax professionals involved in the process because they can appreciate the sensitivities of the questions that are being asked and the tax implications of the information you are providing. In addition, they can often spot an issue before it comes to the attention of the auditor, and help develop a strategy to deal with it, present it to the examiner, and attempt to resolve it early on. You can occasionally build goodwill with an auditor by conceding an issue up front, and then presenting possible solutions. Whatever the situation, it can be important to build trust and credibility with the auditor to the extent that you can; again, this is best done by being timely and open in your responses, while understanding that you do not want to volunteer information they are not asking for.

## Overcoming Obstacles and Challenges

Clients frequently complain about long lapses of time between the commencement of an audit and its conclusion—i.e., significant periods of time may elapse between the time the taxpayer is notified of an audit and the time that it commences. There may also be long periods of time between the conclusion of the audit and the presentation of the proposed adjustments. This does not lend itself to efficient disposition of the cases for either the client or the Commission.

## Triggers for a Tax Investigation

An agency investigation may be triggered by various circumstances. For example, if you have a significant drop in income or capital invested in the state they will look at that situation to see if there has been any planning involved—i.e., any intentional steps to reduce your income in the state or the capital invested in the state. Mississippi has both an income and franchise tax, the latter of which is based on capital invested in this state, and regulators will notice any changes in those areas and will want to know why they occurred. Regulators will also look closely at related party transactions such as royalties paid to an affiliate intangible holding company, or other markers of the type of planning that shifts income out of the state.

Like most states, Mississippi generally follows federal law, but there are significant differences. Mississippi examiners will be looking at your returns to make sure these differences are properly taken into account. For example, Mississippi does not follow federal law that allows taxpayers to claim bonus depreciation equal to 50 percent of certain assets' cost in the year the asset is placed in service. Mississippi has announced by regulation that it will impose penalties if the taxpayer does not make the appropriate adjustments in its Mississippi return to eliminate such bonus depreciation.

Mississippi examiners will also pay close attention to those issues that have no domestic federal tax counterpart, such as how a multistate taxpayer divides its income among the states in which it is doing business

## Final Thoughts

When there is not a lot of money involved, or if the client has a routine issue that the Tax Commission deals with on a frequent basis, we can usually get the matter resolved fairly quickly. However, if we are dealing with a complex fact situation, a significant amount of money is involved, or if there is no real precedent in the law, then a tax matter may become very involved. Tax issues are always easier to resolve when both the client and the Commission want a matter to be resolved fairly and equitably, and are willing to work toward a resolution.

Since there is not a great volume of published Mississippi tax law, I always advise clients who will be filing tax returns in this state, or who may be facing potential tax law issues, to call a professional and ask questions in advance. A little planning can go a long way in this area, and you can avoid some important pitfalls.

Looking ahead, the governor has recently named a tax study committee to look at all of Mississippi's tax laws, and we are certainly interested in what comes out of that process. I am always interested in following case law, and any new developments in the legislature with respect to any tax items that may be on the agenda. In addition, I always have my ear to the ground with respect to hot issues for auditors and what they are doing on appeals, because I believe that is an important part of staying current and relevant in this area.

*Louis G. Fuller joined Brunini, Grantham, Grower & Hewes PLLC in 1985 and is now the firm's senior tax attorney, with broad experience in individual and corporate taxation, including income and transfer taxes. In addition, a significant portion of his practice involves state and local taxation, where he represents both Mississippi and non-Mississippi individual and corporate taxpayers in administrative and judicial appeals of state and local income, franchise, sales, use, and property tax assessments. He also advises clients on available tax incentives for new and expanding businesses in Mississippi.*

*Mr. Fuller is a member of the Hinds County, Mississippi, and American Bar Associations and has been an active member in the Taxation and Estates and Trusts*

*Sections. He is a former chair of the Section of Taxation of the Mississippi Bar Association. Mr. Fuller is also a member of the Mississippi Society of Certified Public Accountants and has been a trustee and chairman of the Mississippi Tax Institute, an affiliate of the Society. He is currently an advisory board member of the Paul Hartman Institute on State and Local Taxation, Nashville, Tennessee, and a member of the National Association of Bond Lawyers. Mr. Fuller is also a frequent speaker on taxation topics at Mississippi Bar programs, Mississippi Society of CPA programs, and other seminars.*

*Mr. Fuller graduated in 1975 from the University of Mississippi with a degree in accounting and in 1980 from Southern Methodist University Law School. He is a certified public accountant.*

# Working With State and Local Government Agencies

Jaye Andras Calhoun

*Member*

McGlinchey Stafford PLLC

ASPATORE

## Tax Planning versus Tax Controversy: Different Approaches

Clients seeking help generally fall into one of two categories: they need help with tax planning issues or resolving tax controversies. When a client is in the planning phase of a project, an informed, conservative approach tends to avoid problems later on. Clients need to know what the tax consequences are and, if possible, how to structure a transaction for optimal tax consequences consistent with their business goals while avoiding unnecessary negative tax consequences. Effective representation when providing advice in a tax planning context involves anticipating trouble and steering clients clear from the very beginning. Think of everything that can go wrong and take action in advance. Although "tax planning" has a negative connotation in the view of state and local tax administrators, this is unfortunate because a business can only be successful to the extent that management considers all financial issues that impact the bottom line, including tax issues, and seeks out and implements appropriate advice. Assuming a client does not wish to travel to extremes in erecting tax structures that have little or no economic substance and resemble nothing so much as tax avoidance, it only makes good business sense to think through any possible tax consequences before entering into a transaction.

Tax controversies generally arise when the deal has been closed, the transactions are completed and the client has been conducting business for a period of time so that the operative facts are in place. Clients may seek advice and ask questions based on an anticipated audit or an audit in progress. In some cases, clients believe that they are going to be able to resolve a tax issue at the audit stage and are surprised to learn, only on the issuance of an unfavorable assessment, that the auditor either did not agree with them or used information provided by the client to arrive at a determination that additional tax is due based on factors that the client did not anticipate would generate additional liability.

When it's clear that a tax controversy has arisen, the focus shifts to trying to mitigate damage and determining how to handle the audit or litigation in order to best achieve this minimization. Clients may need assistance in contesting audit issues or disputing a proposed or final assessment on factual and/or legal grounds. Good representation involves assisting clients to present appropriate information as well as making relevant arguments clearly and at the earliest stage so as to minimize time and expense. Although it is the rare client who clearly has no possible factual and legal defense to issues raised in audit or in litigation, that client should be advised as to potential exposure and options for payment of tax liabilities should be discussed. All other clients (those with legitimate factual or legal grounds for contesting the assessment) should be guided in presenting those arguments, and persisting in making those arguments, to the point where the optimal resolution can be reached. With respect to all clients, procedural issues should be considered early in the process to determine whether any relief is available on procedural grounds (such as the expiration of a statute of limitations or failure of the taxing authorities to follow relevant statutes and ordinances). It is imperative that procedural issues be raised on a timely basis.

After planning and controversy issues have been resolved, it is important to ensure that all parties to the transaction or to the controversy (and all relevant client personnel) understand how the issues were resolved and how the same or similar transactions should be treated in future operations. Within a business, it will be important to institute policies and procedures to report income, for example, or to collect sales or use tax, consistent with how a transaction was structured or based on what was learned in an audit or based on the terms of a settlement resolving litigation. Also, government agencies frequently have difficulty modifying internal systems to reflect the terms of a settlement so it is important to monitor any correspondence from the agency after the resolution of the case to ensure that appropriate controls are put in place. Effective representation involves assisting the client with establishing policies and procedures going forward as well as following up with state and local tax authorities to ensure that the terms of a settlement or administrative or court decision are followed.

## Tax Advice: Common Client Issues

### *Combating the "Brother-in-Law" as Tax Adviser*

Clients are best served by receiving timely and accurate information from their representatives. Clients have been known to say with absolute certainty that a certain tax treatment is appropriate on the authority of the client's brother-in-law who has been doing it that way for years. Also, businesspeople frequently have an understanding of tax rules based on the way the industry has always done it and may not be aware of new legislation or court cases that change the rules or of a shift in administrative policy on the part of the tax collector—which can cause problems in audit situations. A recent client, for example, faced a large audit assessment based on an industry practice that has always been inconsistent with state law but which, until recently, wasn't enforced by the state department of revenue. Industry employees have understood the rules incorrectly for so long that reeducating them has presented an uphill struggle on a steep learning curve: "yes, although everyone in the industry understands 'x' to be the rule, the government has only now increased scrutiny of the practice and is only now starting to issue assessments for back taxes."

*Going to the Source*

The Department of Revenue of the State of Louisiana has adopted La. Admin. Code §61:III.101 which provides guidelines for the issuance of administrative rules and other types of policy statements as well as private letter rulings directed to particular taxpayers upon request. To its credit, the Department issues rules and other policy statements that are intended to "provide guidance as to the Department's position and ensure that employees enforce the tax laws correctly, consistently, and fairly." La. Admin. Code §61:III.101(A) (2001). Many states have similar procedures for issuing public guidance as well as private letter rulings which will outline the state's view as to the tax treatment of a specific anticipated transaction. Localities may also provide information based on a specific set of facts to a taxpayer requesting such advice but it is unlikely that there will be a formal procedure for requesting such advice—usually a letter will do. In the right situation in which the client has the time to seek formal advice and there is enough money at issue, it may be appropriate to seek a private letter ruling on behalf of the client. Such formal advice is useful when the tax consequences of an anticipated transaction are not clear and it is important to know, in advance, how the Department will view the applicable law. The taxpayer is required to provide all relevant facts when requesting a private letter ruling and the Department will not be bound by its opinion if it is determined at a later date that significant facts were not disclosed. A copy of the Louisiana Department of Revenue's requirements for requesting a private letter ruling is attached as Appendix E. *See* http://revenue.louisiana.gov/sections/lawspolicies/request-plr.aspx.

*Reviewing All Relevant Information*

In order to provide accurate and useful tax advice to a client, a lawyer should understand as thoroughly as possible (commensurate with the scope of the representation) the client's business. Understanding a client's business starts with asking open-ended questions and ideally involves reviewing original documentation to confirm that the documents say what the client thinks they say and to spot unnoticed issues. With respect to some clients, it makes sense to tour the client's facilities. At a minimum, an attorney should review the information available on the client's Web site and, sometimes, the Web sites of a client's competitors. Some clients are surprisingly reluctant to provide information even to their attorneys, perhaps concerned about costs, or misguidedly believing that if the attorney doesn't know about unfavorable information, the Department of Revenue will be less likely to discover it. While it is critically important to keep in mind a client's budget, it is also critically important for the attorney to either obtain all information necessary to provide accurate advice, or, at a minimum, to advise the client as to the limitations of the advice—after all, the attorney's recommendations can only be based on the information available to the attorney. A client's (and the client's attorney's) credibility is damaged to the extent a tax collector is able to bring damaging information to the attention of the client's representative when the client should have mentioned it to the attorney first. A recent collection client, an individual, was surprised to learn that the Department of Revenue's collection division has access to the state's motor vehicle records. Fortunately, we were able to provide documentation showing that the client had donated the vehicle in question to one of his children many years earlier and that the child had failed to transfer the title on the public records—so the client had reasonably failed to disclose his ownership of the vehicle on the collection information statement he filed as part of an offer-in-compromise.

Once the representative has established a thorough understanding of the operative facts of the client's business, a representative must then understand the audit history and what took place with the auditor in the immediate past—attorneys, after all, are not usually involved at the front end of the audit. At the point that the attorney gets involved, much useful information is available because of reviewing the documentation that has already been provided to the auditor, reviewing client notes reflecting what representations were made by the client, and asking detailed questions about what the client believes the auditor's position is. Ask about the series of events that led to the present audit. Find out what the client views as an optimal outcome and advise the client as to whether the client's wishes are realistic or if there are favorable options the client has not previously considered. In a sales or use tax audit, for example, it may not be enough to simply advise the client to start collecting tax from customers; most businesses are reluctant to collect and remit tax when their competitors are not—it puts them at a competitive disadvantage. In order to give the client useful advice, it is important to know how such advice might impact a client's competitive bottom line—while, on the one hand, if the Department of Revenue has begun auditing the whole industry, then collecting the tax from customers may not be an issue for the client, but most businesses do not wish to be the first in their field to start collecting the tax.

It is important, when clients receive audit work papers, to review them carefully to understand the auditor's theory of the case and whether they had before them sufficient and correct information to base the assessment on. In one recent case, a review of the auditor's work papers revealed that the auditor, who believed he was asking for a certain type of invoice, had, in fact, received something very different from the client, and made an assumption based on the information received that a large amount of client transactions were taxable, when in fact they were not. Mistakes and miscommunications are not uncommon and can sometimes be remedied as a result of carefully analyzing the auditor's work papers and the source documents on which they are based.

## Common Client Issues in Tax Audits

Client issues break down into either factual or legal issues or a combination of both. Factual issues tend to be easier to resolve at the audit stage than legal issues. Legal issues, involving a true disagreement on the law (rather than a situation in which the auditor simply has overlooked an aspect of the applicable law and is willing to concede the point once the relevant provisions or jurisprudence is brought to his or her attention), are not usually resolved at the audit stage.

*Factual Issues: The Right Documentation Goes a Long Way*

Factual issues frequently are resolved by providing documentation to the auditor in support of the client's position but, as always, the "devil is in the details." Substantiation of a taxpayer's position through providing documentation can take the form of providing copies of the relevant books and records of the business or, in some cases, obtaining information that tends to support the client's position from third parties or even providing affidavits from knowledgeable persons.

In one recent case, the client was able to create documentation that supported its position, which documentation was accepted by the Department of Revenue as well as local taxing authorities. That case involved an out of state business that had been selling products over the Internet and by mail to Louisiana residents. The client took the position that it had no nexus with the state but the Department of Revenue disagreed and argued that the client should have been collecting and remitting use tax on its sales to Louisiana residents. The client sold its product to both business and individual purchasers and suspected that many of its business clients would have self-accrued and remitted taxes on these purchases. The case was settled based on statistics compiled while the case was in litigation. The client researched its records and identified all business customers having made purchases in amounts greater than a threshold amount during the tax years in litigation. The client was then willing to send out surveys to its customers explaining briefly the reason for the inquiry and asking the customer to reply as to whether the client believes it paid use tax on the purchases. Surprisingly, a substantial number of the client's business customers returned the survey. Almost all of the customers responding (not surprisingly) reported that use tax had been remitted on these purchases and some even provided proof. The Department of Revenue allowed the results of the survey to reduce the tax liability at issue based on the percentage of business clients who said they had self-reported and remitted the use tax. Since such taxes are designed to be collected only once, these efforts substantially reduced the client's ultimate liability. Although other clients have been unwilling to consider contacting their customers in this manner, it is important to remember in cases involving dealer liability that the dealer's customers may have already paid the tax at issue and to consider creative ways of substantiating this likelihood so as to reduce your client's exposure.

Although document production has traditionally consisted of compiling huge packages of source documents, client work papers, and spreadsheets and mailing or hand delivering this information to the taxing authority after reviewing it, much of this information may now be transmitted in electronic form. It is now common to receive information instantaneously over the Internet and information can be transmitted to auditors in much the same way. A client recently sent me an e-mail with four spreadsheets containing a substantial amount of information and sent a disk over night with the business' general ledger for me to review as backup. While this new ease with which large amounts of information can be transmitted is useful, at the same time, an attorney may no longer simply follow the "paper trail" in identifying information relevant to an audit or in litigation. It is important to review information contained in the client's electronic data storage and retrieval systems, which may require some additional expertise.

*Legal Issues: Auditor's Have Limited Flexibility*

Every attempt should be made to discuss legal issues with an auditor to ensure that the auditor is aware of all applicable client-favorable law, however, many audits involve differences of opinion on legal issues. Legal disputes cannot always be resolved at the audit level. An auditor may simply be carrying out the Department's latest industry-specific policies and he or she may be constrained by the requirement to follow the Department's official position on an issue. In the absence of specific pronouncements from the taxing authority, many auditors seem to feel that it is their duty to resolve legal gray areas in favor of taxation and no amount of argument will sway them from this course. In all cases, the best way to win a legal argument with an auditor is to find a specific Department policy document that supports the taxpayer's position. If such a document does not exist, one can always argue case law interpreting a statute or a constitutional provision and hope that it is a judicial decision with which the taxing authority agrees. In Louisiana, it is not uncommon to hear tax auditors at the local level say that they just don't agree with the decision in a court case, even if the case is directly on point. In any event, if the auditor does not agree and the attorney believes the auditor is interpreting the law incorrectly, in some cases it is advisable to ask for a meeting with the auditor's reviewer. The Department will not issue a private letter ruling with respect to an issue under audit. Although Louisiana has a pre-payment forum for certain tax issues, the Board of Tax Appeals, taxpayers are not always afforded the opportunity to appeal to the Board of Tax Appeals as access is controlled by the Department. If a client is unable to resolve a legal issue with the auditor and is willing to follow the procedures for paying the tax under protest (paying tax, penalty, and interest computed to the date of payment) and filing suit on a timely basis (in Louisiana, that's within thirty days of the payment under protest), the client may have more luck arguing the legal issue with the Department's in-house attorneys or contract counsel. An arguable position that may not be clearly strong enough to win a case may nonetheless form the basis of a favorable settlement once the matter is in litigation.

*Controlling the Responsiveness of Requested Information is Critical*

While, the most valuable service a representative can provide for the client is to provide accurate information, a representative can also add value by acting as an intermediary between the client and the taxing authority and controlling the flow of information to the governmental authority. In the large assessment example, the client's in-house staff furnished the auditor with books and records from a much broader range of operations than had been requested by the auditor—and, based on the voluminous information provided unnecessarily, the auditor expanded the scope of her audit and her proposed work papers computed a very large assessment based on her identification of an issue not previously raised. Among other problems, this created internal issues; the client's reserve was based only on the resolution of anticipated issues. Arguably, if a tax professional had been in place to control the flow of information, the client would have been far less likely to end up with that large assessment issued before the statute of limitations on the earliest periods under review expired. It is, of course, a judgment call as to whether the tenor of an audit (from cooperative to overly cautious) might change as the result of the visible involvement of an attorney so, in certain situations, it may be advisable for the attorney to provide advice and review documentation behind the scenes. In the latter case, the attorney should take great care to educate the client's responsible employee as to how to handle interactions with the auditor to be truthful but not to speak outside the employee's sphere of knowledge or responsibility, and to take care to not create any unnecessary additional exposure for the client.

In the tax area, the ability to look at the source documents in the same way that an auditor would is required. Litigators who do not do a lot of tax work and who find themselves handling a tax case can benefit from a good accounting paralegal or someone who can help interpret the information for them. Even experienced tax practitioners can minimize client expense by working closely with a client's tax department. Many of my clients employ in-house accounting and tax professionals who are very helpful in understanding the factual basis for the documentation and support that will be proffered to the auditor. However, the information is analyzed, it is important that tax counsel understand the information before handing the package over to the auditor. By permitting counsel to handle the response to an information production request, the client need not give any more information than has been requested, and may avoid the exposure resulting from an auditing team setting up camp in the client's offices and rummaging through files.

*To Extend or Not to Extend: The Prescription Dilemma*

A common issue that arises in tax audits is whether the client should agree to extend the statute of limitations on assessment. The Louisiana Constitution generally provides that a tax, except a real property tax, prescribes (becomes unassessable) three years after December 31st of the year in which the tax is due, however, the limitations period may be suspended or interrupted so that the prescription date is extended. *See* 1974 La. Constitution Art. VII, §16; La. Rev. Stat. Ann. § 47:1579 (2008). The prescriptive period may be suspended by the issuance of an assessment, the filing of a lawsuit involving the taxes, the filing of a false or fraudulent return, a written agreement to suspend the prescriptive period for the tax year at issue between the taxpayer and the state or the Internal Revenue Service (even if executed only with respect to federal taxes), the start of an IRS audit, the filing of a bankruptcy by the taxpayer or by failure to file a return. Many states have similar provisions.

The decision as to whether to sign an agreement to extend the statute of limitations depends on a number of factors. Overburdened tax officials often request that taxpayers extend the statute of limitations in order to create more manageable workloads for themselves and, in some cases, because the client has not been cooperative. That is, in order to prevent the expiration of the statute of limitations that closes a tax year for purposes of additional assessment of tax, the auditor may require the client to execute a waiver of the statute of limitations. Frequently, audits seem to take more time than they should. After a client's case reaches the top of the auditor's to-do pile (which can take years), the auditor may make multiple requests for information that must then be reviewed only after which can he or she complete work papers, submit them to the taxpayer for comments, review any additional information provided and then repeat until the auditor considers the work finished, and only then will the auditor's findings be submitted to an audit reviewer, which may lead to the issuance of an assessment. The process may take months and clients can become frustrated with repeated requests for extensions accompanied by a failure to conclude an audit on a timely basis because interest is running on any assessment resulting from the audit. Clients may seek professional advice regarding whether to execute a waiver of the statute of limitations where the concern is that the auditor is unreasonably failing to conclude an audit and with the knowledge that extending the statute lessens the incentive for the auditor to "wrap it up."

Considerations that go into deciding whether to recommend signing an extension are varied. If one is convinced that one's case is strong or that the proposed assessment will be reduced substantially once additional information is provided, then signing the waiver makes sense. If, on the other hand, a client has significant exposure in an area outside of the current focus of the auditor, then it might make more sense to simply force the auditor to finalize his or her findings by refusing to agree to an extension—although the client runs the risk that the auditor will simply issue an assessment for the maximum potential amount to protect the taxing authority's interest, such a decision could foreclose auditor inquiries into areas of exposure and put the client in the more defensible position of paying an arbitrary assessment under protest and then providing proof that the assessment is incorrect in the context of litigation. The fact that, if the client disagrees with the assessment, the amount must be paid under protest and any recovery of the funds paid would have to wait, may deter a client from taking the latter course. Because not all states have pre-payment forums where assessments may be contested before a court or administrative body prior to payment, the client's options may be limited to working with an auditor and signing an extension in hopes of minimizing the ultimate assessment or, not signing the extension and allowing the assessment to be issued and then making a payment and taking the assessment to court to decide its accuracy either by a decision of the court or as a result of settlement negotiations with the tax collector's attorneys. When considering the costs of continuing to argue one's case, unfortunately, in Louisiana it should be noted that there are statutes providing for payment of the government's attorneys fees in cases in which the taxpayer is not successful but no comparable statutes providing for payment of a successful taxpayer's attorneys fees.

## Agencies Involved in Tax Issues

### *State Agencies*

In Louisiana, the Department of Revenue has made great strides in being proactive and much more transparent than it used to be. The Department helpfully provides information necessary for taxpayers to be compliant with the tax law and, for the most part, rejects secretive policies. The state could do a better job in some areas, for example, a clear description of the state's nexus standards, for instance, would be helpful to taxpayers. Nonetheless, the Department maintains a fine Web site, places policy documents online, publishes "Tax Topics" which provide much useful information to taxpayers and generally works with taxpayers and counsel—within established limits—commendably to the point where top policy people make themselves available to discuss tax issues.

### *Local Agencies*

Local taxes tend to include property taxes and sales and use taxes. No Louisiana parish is authorized to impose an income tax although many impose occupational license taxes. Local assessors determine the value of real property and business taxpayer's self-report personal property values. With respect to real property, the work product of the various assessors in the form of assessment information may be available on the Internet although this information is not always current. The assessors are subject to the rules and regulations of the Louisiana Tax Commission that are published on the Tax Commission's Web site.

Each parish in Louisiana is required to have one centralized tax collector for sales and use tax purposes. Local governments struggle to raise funds and operate much less formally than the state in their dealings with taxpayers. Although ordinances must underlie all tax assessment and collection activity, there is a dearth of publicly available information. While local tax authorities are usually willing to provide copies of ordinances on request, a call to the tax collector for such information may also include a conversation in which the requesting party will be questioned as to the purpose of the call, the identity of the taxpayer concerned with the ordinances, and other information that should not have to be disclosed in the context of learning what the law of a locality is. Some online services such as www.municode.com provide information but the information is not necessarily current and may include different numbering than the local ordinances relied on by the taxing authority. How local officials may interpret these ordinances can be anyone's guess, therefore, it is important to develop a good working relationship with local tax officials. Some local officials are more litigious than others are. Many local tax collectors hire outside auditing firms to perform contract audits. These auditors appear to be paid on a contingency basis (or perhaps their contracts are renewed on the basis of the dollar amount of proposed assessments—which creates significant conflict of interest problems and is inconsistent with principles of governmental independence and integrity), but even in these cases the collector has the final say and so may be appealed to. A recent client, for example, was audited by an outside contracting firm that was particularly unwilling to allow the client, a Fortune 500 company, the benefit of the doubt for any item of substantiation that the auditor did not see with his own eyes. The client had so many different problems with the contract auditing firm that we visited the collector and directly pleaded our case: the outside agency is forcing the business to prove every item rather than taking a more practical approach which might include a statistical sampling to reduce the burden of the audit on this large company. The client was simply unable to produce the enormous volume of records required to satisfy the outside auditor quickly enough and the auditor proposed an assessment that was so inaccurate that it would surely be thrown out of court once additional information could be provided. The collector was ultimately satisfied with the inaccuracy of the proposed assessment and required the auditor to take additional time to review the client's records at a more realistic pace. After persevering, the audit concluded with an assessment that was half of the original proposed assessment.

## Current Trends in Tax Assessment

The biggest issue in state and local tax right now is an increasing willingness on the part of tax collectors to assert that nonresidents have "nexus" (a sufficient connection with the state to support the state or local government's right to exercise taxing jurisdiction over the nonresident) in situations that would not have been considered sufficient in the past. Once, before a state would require a nonresident vendor to collect and remit its taxes, the taxpayer would have to have some physical presence in the state, such as a bricks-and-mortar building or employees who come into the state or the presence of company trucks regularly within its borders making deliveries. Today, states have been stretching the boundaries of what has traditionally been considered nexus and finding "connections" through a nonresident's contractual relations with in-state residents and because states have been increasingly adopting a concept of "economic nexus" such that if a nonresident taxpayer receives income from in-state residents then that is sufficient to provide nexus. Taxpayers are hoping for relief in the form of congressional legislation or a Supreme Court opinion to curb the expansion of the concept of "economic nexus" as such a standard is, essentially, no standard at all. While such a concept has the advantage to in-state governments of seemingly exporting the tax burden to the extent that nonresidents are not voters and seem to have little sympathy in the state's courts, this unfortunate trend is causing significant consternation to the taxpayers operating in interstate commerce and finding themselves, without notice, at the mercy of far-flung tax jurisdictions proposing substantial assessments based on a revisionist view of the relevant law.

*Jaye Calhoun is a member in McGlinchey Stafford PLLC's New Orleans office. She has served as chair of the Louisiana State Bar Association Section on Taxation in 2004 to 2005, and is currently the chair of the New Orleans Bar Association Tax Law Committee. Ms. Calhoun is a member of the Executive Committee of the State and Local Tax Subcommittee of the American Bar Association's Section on Taxation and heads up the SALT committee's business activity taxes and nexus White Paper task force. She is board-certified in tax and estate planning and administration by the Louisiana Board of Legal Specialization, and is a former attorney for the Internal Revenue Service.*

*Ms. Calhoun has spoken to numerous professional and community groups on tax-related issues. She is a frequent contributor to professional publications and has served as a Louisiana contributor to the American Bar Association's "State and Local Tax Lawyer" and has contributed to Lexis-Nexis "Practice Insights" on Louisiana law. Ms. Calhoun has co-authored several books on taxation and dealing with tax agencies and has written numerous articles on recent developments in taxation. Ms. Calhoun is an adjunct professor at Loyola Law School where she teaches a course in state and local taxation.*

*Ms. Calhoun's practice in the business section focuses on state and local taxation and regulatory issues, nonprofit and health care related tax issues, estate planning and planned giving, business planning and formation as well as tax audits and tax litigation.*

*Ms. Calhoun received her LL.M. from Georgetown University Law Center, LL.M., her J.D. from Tulane Law School, and her B.S. from H Sophie Newcomb Memorial College of Tulane University.*

*Ms. Calhoun has been recognized in* The Best Lawyers in America ® *(Tax Law) and* Louisiana Super Lawyers *(Tax). She is a Martindale-Hubbell AV Peer Review Rated Lawyer.*

# APPENDICES

# Appendix A

# OVERVIEW OF PENNSYLVANIA STATE AND LOCAL TAXES

## MEMORANDUM

Joseph C. Bright May 4, 2007

This Memorandum summarizes the highlights of Pennsylvania state and local taxes likely to be of interest to business organizations, particularly foreign organizations coming into the Commonwealth of Pennsylvania.*

## I. Introduction

The principal Pennsylvania taxes include: two major taxes on businesses; specialized taxes imposed on certain industries; a sales and use tax and other consumption taxes; a personal income tax; a realty transfer tax; and miscellaneous other taxes. Noteworthy features of these taxes are that Pennsylvania does not tax corporations on a unitary basis, its historically troublesome Capital Stock Tax is scheduled to be phased out, and the Personal Income Tax rate is low and the tax simple compared to other states. These and certain other features of various state taxes are discussed briefly below.

---

* For further and more current details, and for coverage of other Pennsylvania taxes, the reader is referred to the author's treatise, *Taxation*, published by West Group as volumes 26 and 27 of *Summary of Pennsylvania Jurisprudence 2d.*

Taxing powers have been delegated by the Commonwealth to counties, municipalities, school districts, and certain other local jurisdictions. They impose real property taxes and various other taxes, including gross receipts taxes on businesses and realty transfer taxes. Philadelphia taxation is unique in many respects and includes several specially tailored taxes.

II. Pennsylvania Taxes

A. Principal Business Taxes. Pennsylvania imposes three taxes on corporations generally:

- Corporate Net Income Tax (CNI Tax)
- Capital Stock - Franchise Tax
- Corporate Loans Tax

The CNI Tax is a tax on net income. The Capital Stock - Franchise Tax is in the nature of a net worth tax, and the Corporate Loans Tax is an anachronistic tax on interest paid to Pennsylvania residents with respect to certain corporate debt obligations.

1. CNI Tax. The CNI Tax is adapted from a model tax (UDITPA) on net income. It is imposed at the rate of 9.99%. The tax is imposed on the taxpayer's separate company federal taxable income after certain adjustments and after allocation and apportionment, if applicable.

CNI taxpayers are corporations carrying on activities in Pennsylvania, no matter where incorporated. Taxpayers include those limited liability companies, business trusts and partnerships that are treated as corporations for federal income tax purposes, but do not include certain business trusts that qualify as regulated investment companies (RIC), real estate investment trusts (REIT), and related entities. In addition, banks, certain other financial institutions, and insurance companies are not taxpayers. Taxpayers do not include trusts (other than business trusts) and other entities that are not treated as corporations for federal income tax purposes.

A multi-member limited liability company that is classified as a partnership for federal tax purposes is treated as a partnership for CNI Tax purposes, while a single-member limited liability company that is classified as a disregarded entity for federal income tax purposes is treated as a disregarded entity for CNI Tax purposes. Thus, neither is subject to the CNI Tax. However, all limited liability companies, regardless of federal classification, are subject to the Capital Stock-Franchise Tax.

For tax years beginning on or after January 1, 2006, a corporation that has elected under federal income tax law to be treated as an S corporation is also treated as an S corporation for Pennsylvania purposes unless it elects to be treated as a C corporation. For tax years beginning before January 1, 2006, a separate Pennsylvania S election was required. A Pennsylvania S corporation is not subject to the CNI Tax, except as to built-in gains; rather the shareholders are subject to the Personal Income Tax, discussed below. A Pennsylvania S corporation is nonetheless subject to the Capital Stock - Franchise Tax.

The base of the CNI Tax is federal taxable income determined on a separate company, unconsolidated basis. Generally, federal law governs what is included in the base. Pennsylvania adds back all taxes based on or measured by net income. The tax base does not include dividends received from other corporations to the extent the dividends are deducted for federal income tax purposes, with parallel deductions for dividends from foreign corporations. A corporation can deduct interest and gains received from United States obligations less certain related interest expense.

A CNI Tax taxpayer that is taxable by both Pennsylvania and another jurisdiction may allocate and apportion its CNI Tax base. Allocation is a process in which selected items of income are attributed entirely to one state. Few, if any, items of income are likely to be allocated under Pennsylvania law. The balance of federal taxable income is apportioned by a formula that averages three factors, one for each of tangible property, payroll, and sales, with the sales factor 70% weighted. In each case, the numerator of the factor consists of items attributable to Pennsylvania, and the denominator consists of all such items.

Net operating losses can be carried forward for 20 years for CNI Tax purposes up to a maximum deduction of the greater of $3 million per year and 12.5% of the company's taxable income.

A number of other states impose taxes on corporations on a *unitary* basis. Under unitary taxation, the taxable income of a corporation that is a member of a group of corporations constituting a unitary business is defined as the income of the entire group. The taxpayer's income is then apportioned using factors based on the entire group. Pennsylvania does not tax income on a unitary basis. However, Pennsylvania courts on occasion apply the reverse of unitary taxation, called *multiform taxation.* Under multiform taxation, a corporate taxpayer conducting more than one distinct business, only one of which is conducted in Pennsylvania, is taxed only with respect to its Pennsylvania operations.

2. Capital Stock - Franchise Tax. Technically, the tax is two taxes: The Capital Stock Tax is imposed on all domestic corporations, and the Franchise Tax is imposed on foreign corporations carrying on activities in Pennsylvania. In almost all other respects the taxes are identical.

The tax is imposed for tax years beginning in 2007 at the rate of 3.89 mills (.389%) on *capital stock value*, after any applicable apportionment. The tax rate is scheduled to be reduced in yearly increments until it reaches zero after 2010. Most taxpayers for CNI Tax purposes are also taxpayers for purposes of the Capital Stock - Franchise Tax. However, all LLCs and business trusts are taxpayers, no matter how they are treated federally, except for certain REIT- and RIC-related business trusts. A Pennsylvania S Corporation is liable for the Capital Stock - Franchise Tax, even though it is not a taxpayer for CNI Tax purposes.

Capital stock value is determined by averaging two components, less a deduction. The first component is 75% of book net worth as reflected on the corporation's federal income tax return. The second component is the average of the last five years of book net income as reflected on the federal income tax return, capitalized at 9.5%. Capital stock value is the average of the two components, less $125,000.

Two apportionment options are available. A corporation entitled to allocate and apportion for CNI tax purposes may apportion its capital stock value by a three-factor formula that is constructed the same as the CNI Tax formula, except that the sales factor is not extra-weighted. A manufacturer or processor can exclude from the numerator of the property and payroll factors (but not the sales factor) items attributable to manufacturing. Alternatively, a corporation may elect a unique Pennsylvania single-factor asset apportionment formula. The single factor is: taxable assets divided by all assets. Unlike three-factor apportionment, assets for purposes of single factor apportionment include both tangible and intangible assets. All intangible assets, unless otherwise exempt, are attributable to Pennsylvania (*i.e.* included in the numerator) regardless of where the taxpayer is domiciled. Some of the assets that are exempt, and therefore excluded from the numerator, are:

- real and tangible property located out of Pennsylvania
- assets devoted to manufacturing in Pennsylvania
- obligations of the United States or of Pennsylvania
- stock in Pennsylvania corporations
- stock in any corporation owned to the extent of more than 50 percent

A taxpayer may make an annual election to use either three-factor or single-factor apportionment. Additionally, a taxpayer qualifying as a *holding company* under a statutory definition may use a special 10% apportionment factor. Other options are available for certain specialized industries.

3. Flow-Through Nexus. Provisions in both the CNI Tax and Capital Stock - Franchise Tax state that a corporation's interest in an entity which is not a corporation for purposes of the

particular tax is considered a direct ownership interest in the assets of the subordinate entity. Consequently, a corporation, not otherwise present in Pennsylvania, that has a interest in a partnership (or other entity not treated as a corporation for purposes of the particular tax) that is present in Pennsylvania is taxable in Pennsylvania.

4. Corporate Loans Tax. The Corporate Loans Tax is imposed on interest paid by certain corporations to Pennsylvania residents. The tax is imposed at the rate of 4 mills on the *nominal value* of the debt obligation, which is the amount of interest paid divided by the interest rate. Generally, nominal value will be face value. A Pennsylvania corporation and a foreign corporation with its treasurer located in the Commonwealth must withhold the tax. As a matter of practice, most corporations do not withhold the tax, but pay it from their own funds.

Other Business Taxes. Pennsylvania imposes various taxes on specialized forms of businesses. Banks, trust companies, and title insurance companies located here are taxed under the

The Public Utility Realty Tax (PURTA) is imposed by Pennsylvania on real estate owned by utilities, in lieu of local real estate taxes. After 1999, electric generation facilities are taxed locally, not under PURTA.

B. Consumption Taxes. Pennsylvania imposes several consumption taxes, the most significant of which is the Sales and Use Tax.

1. Sales and Use Tax. The Sales and Use Tax is imposed at the rate of 6% on the value of tangible personal property and certain services sold at retail or purchased at retail and used in Pennsylvania. The tax historically was imposed on a limited class of services related to tangible personal property, principally for the repair, alteration, or maintenance of tangible personal property. A few other services are taxable, including:

- adjustment, collection and credit reporting services
- employment, help supply, secretarial, and editing services

- building and lawn maintenance services
- lobbying services

Employee compensation costs are not included in the tax base of help supply or interior building cleaning services. No tax is imposed on the services of an employee rendered to an employer. The tax was repealed as to computer services in 1997.

In the case of almost all taxable property and services, a purchase for resale is excluded from tax. Thus, no purchaser except the last purchaser in the chain of distribution pays the tax. An exclusion for manufacturing, certain other production activities, and research and development goes beyond the resale exclusion to exclude items of machinery, equipment, and supplies used directly in most production operations. The purchase of tangible personal property not directly and predominantly used in manufacturing (and not resold) generally is subject to the tax.

An exclusion is available for goods sold and delivered out of the Commonwealth, even by a retailer. There are a large number of other exclusions and special provisions.

As with most sales taxes, the tax is imposed on the retail purchaser, but a vendor must collect the tax and remit it to the Commonwealth. A vendor failing to collect the tax is itself liable for the tax.

Philadelphia and Allegheny Counties each impose an additional 1% Sales and Use Tax.

2. Other Consumption Taxes. The Commonwealth imposes several taxes on motor fuels, cigarettes, and alcoholic beverages, all of which generally speaking are imposed only once with respect to any item. The economic burden of each tax is on the consumer.

C. Personal Income Tax. Pennsylvania's Personal Income Tax (PIT) is imposed at the relatively low rate of 3.07%. It is essentially a gross income tax; it does not use federal taxable income as the base.

Taxpayers include resident individuals, estates and trusts, and nonresident individuals, estates and trusts with income from sources within Pennsylvania. Resident shareholders of a Pennsylvania S corporation pay PIT on their entire distributable share of the corporation's income, whether or not distributed. Nonresident shareholders are taxable to the extent that the corporation's income is attributable to sources within Pennsylvania. Partnerships are not taxpayers. Rather, resident and nonresident owners of partnerships and certain other entities treated as partnerships are taxed on a flow-through basis like shareholders in a Pennsylvania S corporation. Resident flow-through entities other than publicly traded partnerships must withhold tax on income distributable to nonresident taxpayers.

D. Transfer Taxes. The Commonwealth imposes a Realty Transfer Tax at the rate of 1% on the transfer of real estate. The tax is imposed jointly on the buyer and seller. The base of the tax is the value of the real estate transferred, without regard to encumbrances. The tax reaches not only transfers of real estate by recorded deed, but also transfers of certain interests in corporations, associations and partnerships owning real estate in Pennsylvania, and certain long-term leases. Most Pennsylvania localities impose an additional realty transfer tax, as discussed below.

Pennsylvania imposes no taxes on mortgages or on the transfer of stock or other securities.

## III. Local Taxes

A. Real Property Taxation. The Commonwealth has delegated the taxation of real property to various classes of localities. Therefore, a landowner may pay taxes to several taxing jurisdictions. The valuation of real estate for all real estate tax purposes is generally administered at the county level. The rate of taxation varies among localities. Generally speaking, the county determines both the fair market value and the assessed value of a parcel of real estate. The assessed value is the fair market value times the *predetermined ratio*, a uniform ratio applied by the county board of assessment to the market value of each parcel of real estate in the county to arrive at assessed value. The tax rate is then applied to the assessed value. An agency of the Commonwealth determines annually the *common level ratio* for each county, which is a statistical determination of the actual ratio of the average of assessed valuation to fair market valuation of real estate taxable in the county. The common level ratio may be substituted for the predetermined ratio in tax appeals under certain circumstances, acting as a rough check on nonuniform assessments in a county.

Manufacturing equipment is ordinarily excluded from the value of taxable real estate. Real estate owned and used by a Pennsylvania institution of purely public charity is exempt from real property taxes.

A 1997 amendment to Pennsylvania's Constitution permits a lower assessment of homestead property.

B. Personal Property Taxation. All counties in Pennsylvania have for several years abandoned the state-authorized personal property tax, in view of the decision in *Fulton Corp. v. Faulkner*, 116 S.Ct. 848 (1996).

C. Other Taxes. A significant number of other taxes are imposed by various Pennsylvania localities. For businesses, the taxes most likely of concern are a mercantile license tax and a business privilege tax. Such taxes are usually imposed as a percentage of the gross receipts of certain businesses.

Most municipalities and school districts impose a realty transfer tax, which beginning October 10, 2005 must conform to the Commonwealth's Realty Transfer Tax (except Philadelphia, discussed below). Generally, the maximum combined rate that can be imposed by a municipality and school district on property within their taxing jurisdiction is 1%. However, home rule municipalities may impose tax at a greater rate. For example, the combined rate for Pittsburgh City and the Pittsburgh School District is 3%.

D. Philadelphia Taxation. Philadelphia taxation is unique in a number of respects. The City and County are merged into one governmental unit. The School District is conterminous with the City and County, and its taxes are administered by the City. The combined taxing power is broader than the power of other municipalities.

1. Business Privilege Tax. The principal Philadelphia business tax is the Business Privilege Tax (BPT). The tax is generally imposed for the tax year 2007 at the rate of 1.54 mills on gross receipts, plus 6.5% of net income. However, special treatment is given to certain classes of taxpayer. Banks and certain other regulated industries pay tax only on the gross receipts component, limited by their net income. Securities dealers pay tax according to a special calculation. Manufacturers, wholesalers, and retailers may elect to be taxed on certain forms of gross profit rather than on gross receipts.

Taxpayers include not only corporations, but virtually all other forms of business entity.

Gross receipts include all receipts from business done in the City. There are a number of different rules for determining what receipts are attributable to City business.

Net income is determined by a one-time election between book income and federal taxable income. The net income of a taxpayer with business operations both in and out of the City may be allocated and apportioned by rules similar to the rules used by the Commonwealth for CNI Tax purposes, discussed above, with the sales factor double-weighted.

Both gross receipts and federal taxable income are subject to certain adjustments. For example, gross receipts do not include receipts from goods sold and delivered outside Philadelphia, nor from certain port activities. Neither do gross receipts nor federal taxable income include certain receipts from affiliated corporations.

2. Sales and Use Tax. Philadelphia imposes an additional 1% Sales and Use Tax on the items that are taxed by Pennsylvania. There are special Philadelphia rules for determining the situs of taxable sales.

3. Business Use and Occupancy Tax. The Philadelphia School District imposes the Business Use and Occupancy Tax on the use of Philadelphia real estate for business purposes, whether the use is by the landowner or by a tenant. The tax is imposed at the rate of $4.62

per $100 of assessed real estate value, payable in monthly installments. The assessed value of Philadelphia real estate for 2007 is 32% of what the City determines to be fair market value. A landlord is required to collect the tax from a business tenant.

4. Income Taxes. The City imposes the Wage Tax on compensation earned in the City, and the Net Profits Tax on net profits earned by unincorporated entities from business conducted in the City. (The Net Profits Tax is in addition to the BPT imposed on net income.) The Wage Tax is imposed in 2007 at the rate of 4.26% on City residents and at 3.7557% on nonresidents. The Net Profits Tax is imposed on profits attributable to residents and nonresidents at the same rates respectively. A credit against Net Profits Tax is provided in an amount equal to 60% of the Business Privilege Tax paid by the taxpayer in the same tax year. The School District imposes a tax on certain investment income received by Philadelphia residents in 2007 at the rate of 4.26%.

5. Other Taxes. Philadelphia imposes real property taxes and a realty transfer tax which is similar, but not identical, to the Commonwealth's Realty Transfer Tax, at the rate of 3%. Thus the combined state and local rate of realty transfer taxation in Philadelphia is 4%.

Philadelphia also imposes several more specialized taxes.

*Courtesy of Joseph C. Bright, WolfBlock LLP*

# Appendix B

# MISSISSIPPI ADMINISTRATIVE RULES

## Title 35 Mississippi State Tax Commission

### Part I Administrative

### Chapter 01 Administrative Practices and Procedures for the Mississippi State Tax Commission

100 Statutory Authority

This Regulation is promulgated pursuant to the authority and requirements of the Mississippi Administrative Procedures Law.

101 Applicability

This Regulation shall be applicable to all matters falling within the jurisdiction of the Commission and the Commissioner except to the extent a statute of the State of Mississippi provides otherwise. This Regulation is in addition to and supplements those statutory provisions which may be applicable.

102 General Purpose

The Agency regulates most tax matters in the State of Mississippi. The Mississippi State Tax Commission's responsibilities also include the regulation of alcoholic beverages, property taxes, motor vehicle tag and titles, issuing permits and certain business registrations. The Commission and Commissioner interpret the statutes that they are charged to administer and enforce.

103 Definitions

When used in this Regulation:

1. "Agency" or "Mississippi State Tax Commission" means the various offices, bureaus, and divisions of the Mississippi State Tax Commission that incorporate the functional duties and responsibilities of the Commissioner as authorized by law.

2. "Commission" means the Chairman of the Mississippi State Tax Commission and the two Associate Commissioners of the Mississippi State Tax Commission.
3. "Commissioner" means the Chairman and Commissioner of Revenue of the Mississippi State Tax Commission.
4. "Denial" means the final decision of the staff of the Agency to deny the claim, request for waiver or application being considered. In this context, staff of the Agency does not include the Review Board or Commission. "Denial" does not mean the act of returning or refusing to consider a claim, request for waiver, or application for permit, title or tag by the staff of the Agency due to a lack of information and/or documentation unless the return or refusal is in response to a representation by the person who filed the claim, request for waiver, or application in issue that information and/or documentation indicated by the staff of the Agency to be lacking and can not or will not be provided.
5. "Last known address," when referring to the mailing of a notice of intent to suspend, revoke or to order the surrender and/or seizure of the permit, tag or title or to the mailing of a denial of permit, tag or title, means the last mailing address of the person being sent the notice as it appears on the record of the agency in regard to the permit, tag or title in issue. All other references to "last known address" mean the official mailing address that the hearing officer, the Review Board or the Commission Secretary has for the addressee in their file on the administrative appeal in which the document or item is being mailed to the addressee. The addressee is presumed to have received any document or item mailed to his official mailing address. It is the responsibility of the addressee to make sure that his official mailing address is correct.
6. "Mail", "mailed" or "mailing" means placing the document or item referred to in First Class United States Mail, postage prepaid, addressed to the person to whom the document or item is to be sent at the last known address of that person. Where a person is represented in an administrative appeal before a hearing officer, the Review Board, or the Commission by a representative, the terms "mail", "mailed" or "mailing" when referring to sending a document or item to that person shall also mean placing the document or item referred to in First Class United States Mail,

postage prepaid, to the last known address of that person's representative. Mailing to the representative of a taxpayer, permittee, tag holder or title interest holder shall constitute mailing and notice to the taxpayer, permittee, tag holder or title interest holder.

7. "Permit" means a type of license or permit that the agency is authorized to issue, suspend or revoke, such as a sales tax permit, a beer permit, a tobacco permit, a dealer license, or designated agent status, but does not include any type of permit issued under the Local Option Alcoholic Beverage Control Law, Section 67-1-1, et seq. or under the Mississippi Native Wine Law of 1976, Section 67-5-1, et seq.

8. "Permittee" means a person holding a permit, applying for a permit or renewing a permit.

9. "Person" means a natural person, partnership, limited partnership, corporation, limited liability company, estate, trust, association, joint venture, other legal entity or other group or combination acting as a unit, and includes the plural as well as the singular in number. "Person" includes the state, county, municipal, other political subdivision and any agency, institution or instrumentality thereof, but only when used in the context of a taxpayer, permittee, tag holder, or title interest holder, or in the context of a person requesting guidance under Section 9 of this regulation.

10. "Refund Claim" means a claim made in writing by a taxpayer and received by the Agency wherein the taxpayer indicates that he overpaid taxes to the Agency and requests a refund of the overpayment and/or a credit against current or future taxes for the overpayment.

11. "Representative" means an individual who represents a person in an administrative appeal before a hearing officer of the agency, before the Review Board, or before the Commission.

12. "Resident," when used to describe a taxpayer or petitioner means a natural person whose residence and place of abode is within the State of Mississippi.

13. "Review Board" means the Board of Review as legally constituted and authorized by statute comprised of those qualified

employees appointed by the Chairman of the State Tax Commission.

14. "Tag" means a type of license tag or plate for a motor vehicle or trailer that the agency is authorized under Mississippi Motor Vehicle Privilege Tax Law, Sections 27-19-1, et seq., or under the Motor Vehicle Dealer Tag Permit Law, Sections 27-19-301, et seq., to issue or approve before issuance, but does not include other types of license tags or plates issued by the county tax collectors except for personalized license tags and only to the extent that the Agency determines under Section 27-19-48 that a personalized license tag applied for is considered obscene, slandering, insulting or vulgar in ordinary usage or demands the surrender or orders the seizure of the tag where issued in error.

15. "Tag holder" means the person in whose name a tag is registered or the person applying for a tag.

16. "Tag penalty" means the penalties imposed under Sections 27-19-63 and 27-51-43 for any delinquency in the payment of motor vehicle privilege tax and ad valorem tax on a motor vehicle which can be waived by the Agency for good reason shown. Pursuant to Section 27-51-103, imposition of this ad valorem tag penalty at the maximum rate of twenty-five percent (25%) also results in ineligibility for the credit against motor vehicle ad valorem taxes provided by that statute. Waiver of the twenty-five percent (25%) delinquency penalty by the agency under Section 27-51-43 shall reinstate credit eligibility.

17. "Tax" means a tax, fee, penalty and/or interest which the agency is required by either general law or by local and private law to administer, assess, and collect.

18. "Taxpayer" means any person or fiduciary liable for or having paid any tax to the Agency.

19. "Title interest holder" means the owner or lienholder in a motor vehicle or manufactured housing as indicated on a title issued by the Agency or as indicated on an application to the Agency for the issuance of a title.

104 Agency Organization

104.01 Functional Duties of the Agency

The Mississippi State Tax Commission is statutorily responsible for the majority of revenue collection activities for the State. The major functional areas of the Agency are identified as follows:

1. Taxation, including but not all inclusive, of the following tax types:
    a. Individual Income
    b. Corporate Income and Franchise
    c. Withholding
    d. Sales and Use
    e. Petroleum
    f. Real and Personal Property
    g. Motor Vehicle Licensing
    h. and other taxes.
2. Business licensing, registration, and permitting of certain businesses.
3. Motor Vehicle Tags and Titles including Interstate and Intrastate Trucking and Motor Vehicle Registration and Titles.
4. Alcoholic Beverages including permitting, liquor distribution, and law enforcement.
5. In addition to the collection of taxes, the Mississippi State Tax Commission determines and certifies to the State Treasurer the tax diversions to counties, municipalities, and such special funds as provided by law within the State of Mississippi.

104.02 Agency Organizational Structure

The following is the Agency organizational structure along with a brief description of the duties and responsibilities of each office:

1. Executive
    a. Legal Division provides legal representation and advice to the Commission, Commissioner, and Agency employees. By and through its attorneys, the division represents the Commission in court cases and before various administrative bodies.

b. Human Resources is responsible for the Agency's personnel system, employee training, development and recognition programs, as well as employee policy development.

c. Communications and Internal Audit is responsible for coordination of communication activities, both internally and externally, and oversight in improving processes and functions through internal audit.

d. Board of Review hears appeals from persons and taxpayers that are aggrieved by certain actions of the Agency.

e. Commission Secretary acts as custodian of books, records and other documents of the Commission, prepares minutes of meetings and orders for matters heard by the Commission, responds to taxpayers and their representatives on tax related questions, assists the Commission in formulating policy, and performs other duties as assigned by the Chairman.

2. Office of Revenue is responsible for administering taxes imposed by the State of Mississippi, registration functions related to taxation, registration and licensing of certain businesses, issuance of motor vehicle titles, economic tax incentives, and issuance of forms.

   a. Income and Franchise Tax Bureau is responsible for administering the Income and Franchise Tax laws of this state. Corporate Division administers Income and Franchise tax laws pertaining to corporations, partnerships, LLC's, and other legal entities. Individual Division administers fiduciary and individual Income Tax laws. Withholding Division administers Withholding Tax laws.

   b. Sales and Use Tax Bureau is responsible for administering the Sales and Use tax laws as well as special county and city levies, Occupancy Tax, Motor Vehicle Rental tax, and the Waste Tire Fee. Contract Branch is responsible for handling issues related to Contractor's Tax on qualifiable construction projects. Post Audit is responsible for issuing late filing penalty notices and performing desk audits of tax returns.

   c. Petroleum Tax Bureau administers tax laws relating to gasoline, special fuels, lubricating oil, compressed gas, natural gas, and the International Fuel Tax Agreement (IFTA).

d. Miscellaneous Tax Bureau is responsible for the administration of various taxes, along with the issuance of licenses, and regulatory oversight for certain business activities including: Privilege Taxes (Insurance Premium, Gaming, Finance Company, and Statewide Privilege for Public Utilities), Excise taxes (Beer and Tobacco), Severance Taxes (Oil, Gas, Timber, and Salt), Estate Tax, Other taxes designated for special funds (Hazardous Waste, Non Hazardous Waste, Public Utility Regulatory, Municipal Gas Regulatory, Railroad Regulation, and E-911).

e. Motor Vehicle Licensing Bureau administers tax laws and fees imposed for use of roads and highways within the State of Mississippi, International Registration Plan for Mississippi-based interstate trucking firms, Motor Vehicle Registration, Motor Vehicle Dealer Registration, and Intrastate Trucking. Additionally, the bureau issues tags and tag decals to the eighty-two (82) counties.

f. Title Bureau administers the Mississippi Motor Vehicle Title Laws and issues certificates of title for motor vehicles and manufactured homes.

3. Office of Audit and Compliance is responsible for performing audits of businesses and individuals, directing compliance activities, collecting delinquent taxes, and assisting businesses in applying for required permits, licenses, and registrations.

a. Criminal Investigations performs investigations of suspected criminal tax evasion.

b. Collections Bureau assists in the collection of delinquent taxes through the issuance of liens, levies, garnishments, and other process.

c. District Service Offices are located in Brookhaven, Columbus, Greenwood, Biloxi, Hattiesburg, Jackson, Meridian, Senatobia, and Tupelo. These offices provide customer service and are home to the Agency's auditors and revenue officers.

4. Office of Administrative Services is responsible for providing administrative and support services for the Mississippi State Tax Commission as well as accounting for the state's tax revenue.

a. Accounting Bureau is responsible for administration of the Agency's budget and ensures that all taxes received by the Agency are properly receipted, deposited, recognized as revenue, disbursed, and reported.
b. Processing Bureau is responsible for the front-end processing of all tax returns and documents and ensures that all returns and payments received by the Agency are properly recorded and deposited.
c. Purchasing Division obtains goods and services and is also responsible for facilities maintenance and security at the Agency's main office.
d. Print Shop Division is responsible for the bulk of all printing requirements of the Agency (including tax forms). The division's mail operations handle the initial receipt of all-incoming mail for the Agency as well as distribution of interoffice mail for the main office. The warehouse is used for storage of forms, supplies, and records for the Agency.

5. Office of Information Technologies is responsible for maintaining computing systems within the Agency.
   a. Infrastructure and Support is responsible for providing and maintaining hardware and existing operating software to support the business operations of the Agency.
   b. Systems Delivery is responsible for systems analysis, development, testing, and deployment of all new application systems in support of Agency's business operations.
6. Office of Alcoholic Beverage Control is responsible for licensing alcoholic beverage retailers, operating as wholesale distributor of alcoholic beverages, enforcement of Mississippi's Prohibition and Local Option Laws, and regulation of the lawful sale of alcoholic beverages.
   a. Permit Branch processes all applications for licensing and, once permits are issued, performs all on-going maintenance to the permit status, bonds, and renewals.
   b. Warehouse stores the alcoholic beverage inventory sold by the Agency and fills and ships orders to licensed retailers.
   c. Purchasing Division is responsible for the registration of spirit and wine vendors and their products overseeing liquor

shipments including special orders into the warehouse and providing inventory control.

d. Enforcement is responsible for enforcement of the Local Option ABC laws, Prohibitions Laws, and certain laws regulating beer.

7. Office of Property Tax is responsible for monitoring the assessments of Ad Valorem value levels and investigating the work product and appraisal methods adopted by the local governing authorities in order for the Commission to equalize the valuation of property throughout the state. (Ad Valorem or property taxes on real and personal property are primarily collected at the local level rather than by the Mississippi State Tax Commission.)

   a. Valuation and Exemption Bureau is responsible for preparing for the Commission's consideration assessments of public service companies, private rail cars, aircraft, mobile homes, motor vehicles, and reviewing industrial tax exemptions to determine if the property qualifies for the exemption.

   b. Homestead Exemption Branch is responsible for reimbursing taxing units of local governing authorities for losses due to the granting of homestead exemptions.

   c. Property Assessment Bureau ensures consistent appraisal and valuation equalization of properties among the municipalities and counties of the state.

105 Obtaining Information

The purpose of this section is to describe how a taxpayer or other interested person may obtain information, other than information concerning proposed rules, from the Agency.

1. Compliance with Mississippi Public Records Act of 1983.

   a. Any person needing to inspect or obtain a copy of any public record in the possession of the Agency must make a written request to the Commission Secretary. The request must describe the record required and whether it is to be provided through either personal inspection or reproduction.

b. Upon receipt of the request, the Agency shall notify the requesting party of the cost or time and place of access to the record. The requesting party must then forward the costs of producing any records. The cost charged is pursuant to a fee schedule established by the Agency. Every reasonable effort will be made to respond to the request within fourteen (14) working days from the date of when the request was made and the fee to produce such record has been paid. Records may not be removed from the Agency for reproduction purposes.

c. If the Commissioner denies the requesting party access to any record, the requesting party will be notified in writing of the cause of denial within fourteen (14) working days from the date of the request.

2. Obtaining copies of tax returns or applications filed with the Agency.

   a. All tax returns, including documents supporting those returns and other tax forms required to be filed with the Agency, are confidential and specific information relating to a particular taxpayer is not public information. The Agency may not release confidential information to anyone other than the taxpayer unless specifically authorized by the taxpayer, statute, or directed to do so by a proper judicial order.

   b. A taxpayer may request a copy of personal filings by submitting a written request. The request must be signed by the taxpayer. In the case of a return of an individual, this request must be signed by that individual. In the case of an income tax return filed jointly, this request must be signed by either of the individuals with respect to whom the return is filed. In the case of a partnership, this request must be signed by any member of the partnership during any part of the period covered by the record requested. In the case of a return filed by a member managed limited liability company, this request must be signed by any person who is a member of the limited liability company. In the case of a return filed by a manager managed limited liability company, this request must be signed by any manager of the limited liability company. In the case of a return of a corporation, this request must be signed by a principal officer of the corporation and attested to by the corporation's secretary or another officer.

c. A taxpayer may request copies of returns to be released to other parties by providing the Agency a signed and notarized document authorizing the release of the document.

d. The written request for copies should be submitted to the Commission Secretary. The written request must include the type of tax return, the tax period(s) requested, and the tax account and/or taxpayer identification number. A fee is charged for the cost of reproducing the copies.

3. Title and Motor Vehicle tag information

a. If a person needs to obtain information from an individual motor vehicle record maintained by the Agency, that person must qualify under the guidelines set by federal statute. The Agency has promulgated Revenue Rule in accordance with the Federal Driver's Privacy Protection Act that protects certain information contained on motor vehicle records. In order to request information, Form 77-600 must be completed and forwarded along with the appropriate fees to the Agency for processing. This form and regulation along with other applicable information is available on the Agency website at www.mstc.state.ms.us.

b. Any title and motor vehicle tag information received by the requesting party is privileged and may not be disclosed to anyone else unless provided for in the rule. Please note that using the information acquired from motor vehicle records for any use other than a permitted use as defined in the rule may subject the offender to criminal fines and other damages.

4. Publications

a. Persons may receive information through instructions included with forms, notices written concerning law changes or procedural changes, booklets, and other publications of the Agency. This information is provided to answer those questions frequently asked but is not intended to be all inclusive. In any situation where the information provided does not adequately address the person's particular circumstances, it is advisable to seek additional guidance.

b. Interested parties may, for a fee, order a copy of these publications by sending a request to the Commission Secretary, however, much of this information may be found free of charge on the Agency's website.

5. Website

a. Statistical information may be obtained from the Agency website. Many forms are available online and may be printed for use.

b. The website also contains links to other websites including links operated by other government agencies, tax related organizations, and tax software providers. The Agency has no control over the content included in websites other than its own.

c. An individual may check the status of an individual income tax refund online. Persons may also check the validity of certain tax permits or licenses on the website.

106 Adoption of Rules and Regulations

106.01 Authority to adopt rules and regulations

The Commission and/or Commissioner are authorized by statute to promulgate rules and regulations consistent and complementary with the law to enforce the laws administered by the Agency. A rule or regulation is a statement of general applicability that implements, interprets, or prescribes policy or describes procedure or practice of the Agency and may include responsibilities of a person not specifically required by statute or by an existing rule or regulation, but this does not include those items excluded in Mississippi Code 25-43-1.102 (i) from the definition of "rule". The terms "rule" and "regulation" are synonymous of each other and the Commission and Commissioner use both terms in referring to the rules they adopt and promulgate. The following discussion of the rule making process applies not only to rules but also to regulations.

106.02 Rule adoption process

With the exception of emergency rules as outlined in Paragraph J of this section, adoption of a new rule or regulation or the amendment of an existing rule is a multi-step process including the following:

1. Drafting the rule or rule amendment.

When the need for a rule or rule amendment is determined, a proposed rule is drafted by Agency personnel for review and discussion with the Commission or Commissioner.

2. Preparing economic impact statement.

   a. An estimate of the costs and benefits to the public, Agency, or to any other government entity of implementing and enforcing the proposed rule and any anticipated effect on state or local revenues will be prepared by the Agency when required and as provided by 25-43-3.105 of the Mississippi Code. A summary of this economic impact statement will be filed with the Secretary of State for publication along with the Commission's or Commissioner's notice of intent to adopt a rule or rule amendment. Any additional information that the Agency determines may be useful will be included in the statement.

   b. An interested party may submit any specific concerns about the economic impact statement during the public comment period to the Agency contact person provided in the notice of intent to adopt a rule.

3. Notice of intent to adopt a rule or rule amendment.

   a. A notice of intent to adopt a rule or rule amendment will be prepared including information pertaining to how interested persons may comment on the proposal. The notice of intent to adopt a rule will include a statement of the purpose and effect of the rule, a summary of the rule and its estimated costs, opportunities for public comment, and the text of the rule.

   b. The notice will be sent to the Secretary of State and to interested parties who are on the Agency Rule Notification Register.

4. Providing opportunity for interested parties to comment.

a. An opportunity for public participation by means of a public comment period will be provided. The notice of intent to adopt a rule or rule amendment will advise the public of its right to comment and provide information concerning how, when, and where to respond.

b. Interested or affected individuals or entities may comment in writing at any time during the public comment period. All written comments should be mailed or delivered to the Commission Secretary within the provided time period for public comment.

c. The Commission or Commissioner may hold a hearing prior to the final adoption of a proposed rule or amended rule. Public comment will be accepted at the hearing as provided in this section. Written comments received or comments made at the hearing are not binding, but will be considered by the Commission or Commissioner in determination of the final form of the rule or rule amendment.

d. The Commission or Commissioner may designate an officer for the purpose of presiding over said hearing and for documenting attendance and comments made. The presiding officer can be a member of the Commission, the Commission Secretary, or an employee of the Agency.

e. The hearing date will be scheduled for a date that is at the minimum twenty (20) days after the notice of the proposed rule is filed with the Secretary of State. The hearing will be open to the public. Anyone wishing to make a presentation at the hearing should notify, in writing, the Commission Secretary no less than seventy-two (72) hours prior to the scheduled hearing time. The written request to speak must include a brief description of the position that will be presented.

f. The presiding officer may limit the time allotted to each speaker. The number of speakers addressing a specific position on an issue may be limited by the presiding officer to prevent undue repetition at the hearing. In the event speakers representing a specific position are limited, the speakers selected to speak to their position will be determined based upon order of receipt of the request. The speaker will be notified of the time allotted and if the speaker is denied due to cause of repetition or failure to timely request opportunity to speak at the hearing.

g. A record of all persons or entities requesting opportunity to speak will be maintained. This record will include the written requests to speak at the public hearing and any denials for cause of repetition or untimely filing of request to participate in the public hearing. All persons participating or unable to participate in the hearing may submit written comments at any time during the public comment period.

h. All persons in attendance will be requested to sign a register to document their attendance at the hearing. A printed agenda including the names of all speakers and their positions on issues concerning the proposed rule will be provided to those in attendance.

5. Filing the rule for adoption

The Commission and/or Commissioner may change, alter, or delete any provisions of the proposed rule after the public comment period unless such change, alteration, or deletion would prevent the rule from being finally adopted per Section 25-43-3.107 of the Mississippi Code. The Commission and/or Commissioner will file the final form of the rule or rule amendment with the Secretary of State. The effective date is thirty (30) days after filing with Secretary of State unless another date later than the required thirty (30) days required is specified in the law or rule.

6. Obtaining information on proposed rule.

a. The Agency will maintain the Agency Rule Notification Register of all persons or entities that have requested notices for all proposed rule changes. The Agency will send notice on all proposed rules or rule amendments to these persons by mail. A fee for this service will be charged for mailing the notice and billing will accompany all notices. A minimum fee of $25 will be charged for each notice that is mailed. Failure to remit the fee as provided will forfeit any future mailings until such fee has been paid. Any interested person may be included on the mailing register for all proposed notices by writing to Commission Secretary. It is a person's responsibility to provide and keep a correct address on file with the Agency.

b. If a person desires notice on all proposed rules and is agreeable to receive the notices by e-mail, there will be no charge for this service. Any interested person may be included on this register by writing to the Commission Secretary. If email preference is not specified, notice will be sent by mail which includes a fee.

c. A person may also request a copy of a proposed rule or rule amendment on a single time basis by contacting the Agency as provided above. For any mailed document, the minimum fee is still applicable.

d. Rule information may also be obtained on the Agency web site.

7. Rule making record

a. The Agency will maintain a current rulemaking docket that contains a listing of the subject matter of possible rules under active consideration within the Agency.

b. The rulemaking docket shall include all information related to the rule in process.

Included will be:

i. The subject matter of the proposed rule,

ii. Reference to all published notices relating to the proceeding,

iii. Where written submissions or written requests for an opportunity to make oral presentations on the proposed rule may be inspected,

iv. The time during which written submissions may be made,

v. Where and when oral presentations may be made,

vi. Where any economic impact statement and written requests of the issuance of other information concerning an economic impact statement may be personally inspected,

vii. The current status of the proposed rule, and

viii. The date of each rule's adoption and when the rule becomes effective.

c. All materials, submissions, reports, and other information that relates to each rule adoption process and procedure will be maintained at the main offices of the Mississippi State Tax Commission and will be available for public inspection by contacting the Commission Secretary.

8. Repeal of a rule

If the Commission and/or Commissioner determine that an existing rule should be repealed, the process followed will be the same procedure as for adoption of a new rule or amendment to a rule.

9. Termination of the proceeding

The Commission and/or Commissioner may determine that the rule or rule amendment should not be adopted after the notice of proposed rule but prior to adoption of the rule. In such event, notice of a termination will be filed with the Secretary of State and notice will be provided to those persons listed on the Agency Rule Notification Register.

10. Emergency rules

   a. The Commission or Commissioner may determine that an imminent peril to the public health, safety, or welfare requires adoption of a rule with less than twenty-five (25) days notice as normally provided.
   b. In such event, the Commission or Commissioner will notify the Secretary of State of the need for an emergency rule, the form of the rule, and the effective dates of the rule. There will be no public hearing or public comment period provided.
   c. The Commission or Commissioner will determine if the need for the emergency rule continues, and if so, will begin the process to adopt the rule permanently as provided in this section.

107 Hearings and Appeals

Effective July 1, 2005, a new statutory uniform administrative and judicial appeal procedure from certain acts of the Agency was established. The administrative appeal process described in this section is based on this new statutory uniform administrative and judicial appeal procedure and is applicable to all administrative and judicial appeals brought under this new statutory procedure. This new statutory procedure is not however applicable to any assessment, refund claim, request for waiver of tag penalty or the suspension, revocation, surrender, seizure or denial of a permit, tag or title or the administrative appeal or judicial appeal thereof where the initial date of said assessment, refund claim, tag penalty, suspension, revocation, denial, surrender or seizure is before July 1, 2005. Anyone seeking an administrative appeal or a judicial review of an action of the Agency where the initial date of the action is prior to July 1, 2005 is directed to consult the applicable administrative appeal and judicial review statutes in effect at the time of the action to determine the proper procedures to be followed and not the provisions of this section.

107.01 Administrative Appeal

This section describes the administrative appeal process applied when a person is aggrieved by certain actions of the Agency. Typically, that action is an assessment of tax when the taxpayer does not agree tax is due; however, the action may also include a denial of refund, assessment of penalties or interest, and other similar items. The intent of the administrative appeal process is to secure a just resolution or decision.

107.02 Administrative Appeal Process

With the exception of an appeal of a tag penalty, this section does not describe the administrative appeal process relating to actions of the Commission and/or the Agency regarding ad valorem taxes and homestead exemption. An administrative appeal from these actions shall be as prescribed by statute. This section also does not describe the administrative appeal process of actions taken by the Commission and/or the Agency under the Local Option Alcoholic Beverage Control Law and/or under the Mississippi Native Wine Act of 1976. The administrative appeal process for such ABC actions is already described in the ABC Regulations of the Commission.

1. Informal Review
    a. The person may seek an informal review of any assessment or other action believed incorrectly issued or any refund improperly denied.

b. In the case when an auditor or examiner determines additional tax is due, the person should first attempt to resolve any questions with the auditor or examiner. If unable to reach an agreement of the audit results with the auditor, a conference with the auditor's supervisor or the supervisor's designee may be arranged. This conference should provide opportunity to both parties to gain a thorough understanding of the basis of the assessment and to make sure that the facts of the case are correct and complete.

c. An informal review may be granted for any situation, but is not required before seeking administrative appeal. The person may continue to attempt to resolve an issue informally with Agency staff once the formal appeal process has begun but the informal review does not toll the time limit to appeal to the Review Board.

2. Representation

A person may represent himself or may choose to have a representative at any point throughout the appeal process. Hearings before the Review Board, a hearing officer, or the Commission are considered confidential and are not open to the public; however, the appellant may permit another person(s) to attend the hearing and to participate as deemed appropriate or necessary.

3. Interest continues to accrue on unpaid balances.

Filing an appeal does not stop interest charges from accruing on any unpaid tax liability. In some situations, penalties may also continue to accrue.

4. Written requests for Administrative Appeal

a. The taxpayer or person appealing must request a hearing in writing. The written request for appeal should include a statement of the relief being sought and the amount of tax, fees, interest and/or penalty, or the action in dispute. The request should also include the tax identification or tax account number, type of tax and tax periods involved, and the reason the taxpayer or person appealing disagrees with the assessment or action.

b. The request must include the person's mailing address and the name and address of his designated representative, if any.

It is the responsibility of the person appealing to provide and maintain an official mailing address on file with the Review Board and/or Commission Secretary. Any change of address during the appeal process must be made in writing and addressed to the body in which the appeal is pending. This address change is for the appeal process only and does not include any address change to tax account information maintained by the Agency.

c. The timeline for appeals are explained further in this section. A request for appeal not received within the time periods provided below will be dismissed.

5. Notice of hearing.

a. A person or the authorized representative will be notified of the hearing by mail at the last known address. The last known address will be the mailing address provided in the written request of appeal.

b. The hearing notice will contain the time, place, and date of the hearing. Notice to the person's or taxpayer's authorized representation constitutes notice to the person or taxpayer.

6. Continuance of hearing

a. A request for a continuance of the hearing will be routinely granted if the request is received within ten (10) days after the notice of the hearing is mailed. If the request for continuance is received beyond ten (10) days, then the determination to continue the hearing will be decided by the Chairman of the Review Board or the Commissioner.

b. The Tax Commission will not be responsible for delay in the delivery of mail.

7. Confidential hearings

All hearings are closed to the public due to the confidential nature of the subject matter. However, through written authorization, the person appealing may waive the right to a closed hearing.

8. Items not subject to appeal.

Items, in general, not subject to administrative appeal include but are not limited to:

a. Certain bond amounts,

b. Penalty rate increases,

c. Declaratory Opinions,
d. Letter rulings,
e. Oral or written advice,
f. Issuance of levy or garnishments,
g. Issuance of liens, warrants or jeopardy warrants, and
h. Diversions or distributions of tax revenue.

9. Request for removal of voting member of appeal board
   a. Any person may request that a member of the voting panel of the Review Board be replaced or a member of the Commission not participate in a hearing if it appears that person's impartiality might be questioned by a reasonable person knowing all the circumstances, or for other grounds.
   b. A written or verbal request for removal of a voting member from the decision process stating the reason the member's partiality is questioned must be made by the taxpayer or person appealing before the commencement of a Review Board hearing. A written request for removal of a member of the Commission from the decision process must be made by the taxpayer or person appealing no more than two (2) weeks after receiving notice of a hearing before the Commission.

10. Timeline for filing appeals
   a. Assessment of tax, denial of refund, or denial of a waiver of tag penalty:
      i. The taxpayer, if aggrieved by an assessment of tax, penalty, interest, a denial of a refund, or by a denial of a waiver of tag penalty, may apply for a hearing before the Review Board. The taxpayer must submit a request in writing to the chairman of the Review Board within thirty (30) days of the date of the action.
      ii. If the Review Board determines that an assessment of tax, penalty or interest is due, the taxpayer must pay the assessment or appeal to the Commission within thirty (30) days from the date of the order of the Review Board. The taxpayer must submit the request for appeal in writing to the Commission Secretary.
      iii. If the Commission determines that the assessment of tax, penalty, or interest is due, the taxpayer must either pay the

tax due or appeal the action to the appropriate chancery court within thirty (30) days of the date of the order of the Commission.

b. Suspension, surrender, seizure or revocation of a permit, tag, or title:

i. If the Agency determines that action against a permit, tag, or title is necessary, the permittee, tag holder, or title interest holder will be notified by mail of the agency's intention to revoke, suspend, or order the surrender or seizure of the permit, tag, or title. The notice will advise the permittee, tag holder, or title interest holder of the time and location for a hearing on the matter that is at a minimum of thirty (30) days from the date of the notice. The hearing will be conducted by the Review Board or by a hearing officer designated by the Commissioner.

ii. If the permittee, tag holder or title interest holder is aggrieved by the determination of the Review Board or hearing officer, the aggrieved party may appeal in writing to the Commission within thirty (30) days of the date of the order. The matter will become final after thirty (30) days if not appealed.

iii. The hearing before the Commission shall be taken down by a court reporter. The order of the Commission shall become final unless the permittee, tag holder, or title interest holder appeals within thirty (30) days from the date of the order in the appropriate chancery court seeking a review of the order.

c. Denial of an application for a permit, tag, or title.

i. If the Agency determines that an application for a permit, tag, or title should be denied, the applicant will be notified either by mail or in person of the Agency's intention to deny the permit, tag, or title. If the denial involves an application for a title, the notice will also be mailed to the designated agent who submitted the title application and any other alleged title interest holders shown on the application. If the applicant or any title interest holder appearing on the application is aggrieved by the denial of application, the aggrieved party shall file a written appeal with the Review Board within thirty (30) days of the notice. The matter will become final after thirty (30) days if not appealed.

ii. If the applicant or the title interest holder remains aggrieved by the determination of the Review Board, the aggrieved party may appeal in writing to the Commission within thirty (30) days of the date of the order. The matter will become final after thirty (30) days if not appealed.

iii. The hearing before the Commission shall be taken down by a court reporter. The order of the Commission shall become final unless the applicant of the permit, tag, or title, or the title interest holder files within thirty (30) days from the date of the order in the chancery court seeking a review of the order.

11. Review Board hearing

a. With exception of matters administered by the Office of Alcoholic Beverage Control and Commission actions related to Ad Valorem Tax, a taxpayer or person in disagreement with an assessment, refund, or other appealable action of the Agency may request a hearing before the Review Board. Three members of the Review Board shall constitute a quorum and may hear any matter before the Review Board; however, an appeal of the intent to revoke, suspend, or order for seizure or surrender of a permit, tag, or title may be heard by a panel of the Review Board or by a hearing officer.

b. Upon timely receipt of a written request from the person appealing or an authorized representative, the Review Board shall promptly schedule a hearing for consideration of the appeal. At the hearing, the Review Board shall decide the issues presented according to applicable law and the facts.

c. A decision in favor of the person appealing may be made without a hearing when the facts are not in dispute, the issues are clearly identified, or the law has been applied to similar situations in previous decisions.

d. There will be no official transcript or recording made of a Review Board hearing. The official record of the hearing will be the minutes and orders of the Review Board which are confidential for all tax matters. Review Board hearings shall be informal and the rules of evidence will be relaxed.

e. The person requesting the hearing or the person's authorized representative will be asked to discuss the facts supporting the claim to provide explanation of how the law supports that claim. Representatives of the Agency may also be asked to discuss the facts in support of the action or cause.

f. The Review Board may request the person appealing the matter or Agency staff to provide additional information and/or documents during the course of its review. Time limits for submission of the additional information or documents will be established by the chair of the Review Board. If the person from whom information or documents are requested fails to respond to the request in the time provided, the Review Board may decide the appeal without the supplemental documents or information.

g. An Order will be issued after the Review Board has fully considered the information provided at the hearing, any post-hearing information, and the laws specific to the case. The chair of the Review Board will prepare the order and mail it to the person or authorized representative. Notice to the authorized representative constitutes notice to the person appealing.

h. The Review Board may elect to uphold the assessment, to amend the assessment, to issue a revised assessment, to issue a refund or credit, to remand the issue to the originating division for further work, or any other action it deems appropriate. If the person remains aggrieved with the decision of the Review Board, the action may be appealed to the Tax Commission.

12. Commission hearing

    a. Any authorized appeal must be timely made to the Commission in writing. The Commission shall consider the appeal request and notify the person appealing or his authorized representative of the time and place fixed for the hearing. Any two members of the Commission constitute a quorum and may hear all appeals.

b. The person or the authorized representative will be asked to discuss the facts and documents in support of the claim and to explain how the law supports that claim. Commission hearings shall be informal and the rules of evidence will be relaxed.

c. The Commission may request the person appealing the matter or Agency staff to provide additional information and/or documents during the course of its review. Time limits for submission of the additional information or documents will be established by the chair of the Commission. If the person from whom information or documents are requested fails to respond to the request in the time provided, the Commission may decide the appeal without the supplemental documents or information.

d. The Commission may elect to uphold the assessment or action, to amend the assessment, to issue a revised assessment, to issue a refund or credit, to remand the issue to the Review Board or originating division for further work, or any other action it deems appropriate. The Commission may also request the person appealing, Agency staff, or both to submit proposed findings of fact, conclusions of law, orders, and/or briefs.

e. After the Commission has fully considered the information provided at the hearing, any post-hearing information, and the laws specific to the case, it shall issue its order conveying its decision in regard to the appeal which order is considered confidential for all tax matters excluding ad valorem tax. The Commission Secretary will mail the order to the person appealing or the designated representative. Notice to the person's authorized representative constitutes notice to the person appealing.

f. In Commission hearings involving tax determinations, the hearing will not be transcribed since any judicial review of the Commission decision will involve a full evidentiary judicial hearing. However, these hearings will be tape-recorded.

g. The Commission hearings regarding beer, tobacco, or sales tax permits, and tag or title matters will be recorded by a court reporter. Hearings before the Commission regarding Alcoholic Beverage Control (ABC) matters shall be held as provided in ABC Regulations.

13. Withdrawal of an appeal
    a. An appeal before a hearing officer, Review Board, or Commission may be withdrawn by the taxpayer or person filing the appeal at any time. The withdrawal may be made voluntarily by the person or may occur involuntarily under the following conditions.
    b. An involuntary withdrawal of an appeal may occur as result of the person failing to appear at a scheduled hearing, failing to timely provide a written appeal in lieu of attendance at a hearing, or by any other act or failure that the body hearing the appeal determines represents a failure on the part of the person to defend his appeal. An involuntary appeal will be documented in the minutes providing the basis of the withdrawal.
    c. A voluntary withdrawal of appeal must be received in writing and sent by the person or authorized representative to the chairman of the Review Board if the appeal is before the Board, or to the Commission Secretary if the appeal is before the Commission.
    d. Following a withdrawal of an appeal, the action shall become final and not subject to further review by the Review Board, Commission or a court. The agency shall then proceed with any action in accordance with the law.
14. Judicial review
    a. Any person aggrieved by the final Order of the Commission may seek a judicial review of that decision as provided by law. The petition shall be filed against the State Tax Commission and must include a concise statement of facts as contended by the person appealing, identify the order from which the appeal is being taken, and set out the type of relief sought.
    b. The petition for a review of an assessment of tax must include a bond double the amount in controversy conditioned to pay the judgement of the court. The bond must be issued by a surety company qualified to write surety

bonds in Mississippi. Alternatively, the taxpayer may pay the assessment, under protest, prior to filing the petition and seek a refund of such assessment.

c. In a petition involving a revocation, suspension, seizure, order to surrender, or denial of a permit, tag, or title, the petition shall contain certification that the petitioner has paid to the Commission Secretary the estimated cost of preparation of the entire record of the Commission on the matter for which a review is sought.

d. The person or the State Tax Commission may appeal an order of the chancery court to the state Supreme Court.

108 Requests for Guidance

1. Any taxpayer or person seeking information concerning their responsibilities and requirements with the laws administered by the Agency may request advice and guidance concerning those obligations. The requests may be through an informal means such as oral advice or letter rulings, or formally through a declaratory opinion.
2. Taxpayers or other persons may also obtain publications of the Agency that provide information useful to complying with the laws administered by the Agency. Most printed publications of the Agency may also be found on the Mississippi State Tax Commission website.

108.01 Oral advice.

1. Many questions may be answered easily over the telephone or in person by an agent of the Commissioner. Advice given at audit meetings or conferences with Agency employees is considered oral advice. Oral advice is considered advisory only and is non-binding.
2. Taxpayers or persons who have complicated questions or issues driven by their own particular business facts and circumstances should seek a letter ruling on the matter or request further advice from the Agency as provided.

108.02 Letter rulings.

1. Taxpayers or other persons may seek guidance by submitting a written request for a letter ruling to the Commission Secretary.
2. When asking for instruction on a specific issue, it is necessary to provide adequate information in order to accurately answer the question. Because the correspondence is based on one person's specific facts and circumstances, the response is restricted to the taxpayer or person making the request for information and the specific facts involved.
3. This written response is considered informal guidance; however, the taxpayer or person requesting the letter ruling may rely on the response absent a law or regulation change and provided that the information presented is factual and complete with no material omissions and no changes have been made with regard to the information provided.
4. If the Agency should at a later date determine that its response was incorrect, the letter ruling will be retracted in writing and the effect of the retraction will be prospective from the date of the retraction letter forward.
5. Notwithstanding a written retraction of the letter ruling, a law or rule change, or the person's particular circumstances altering the issue under discussion, a letter ruling will be valid for a period of seven (7) years from the date of its issuance. At the end of the seven (7) year period, the person should review and update the information in his original request for information and re-submit the question to the Agency.
6. Any letter rulings written by the Agency prior to the adoption of this regulation will be considered valid for a period of seven (7) years from this regulation's adoption date notwithstanding a written retraction of the letter ruling, a law or rule change, or the person's particular circumstances altering the issue under discussion.
7. The Agency will accept anonymous requests for a letter ruling, such as in the case of a voluntary disclosure, but the response will not be binding until the identity of the person has been disclosed to the Agency. The name and other identifying information of the anonymous entity should be provided within ninety (90) days of the date of the letter ruling. The letter ruling

will be considered non-binding if the identity of the entity is not provided within the time period provided.

8. Notice to the person's authorized representative constitutes notice to that person. It is the person's continuing obligation to inform the Agency of the identity and address of its representation.

108.03 Declaratory Opinions.

1. Scope of rules.

These sections set forth the Agency's rules governing the form and content of requests for declaratory opinions, and the Agency's procedures regarding the requests, by Mississippi Code Ann. § 25-43-2.103.

2. Persons who may request declaratory opinions.

Any person with a substantial interest in the subject matter may submit a written request to the Agency for a declaratory opinion by following the specified procedures. "Substantial interest in the subject matter" means that the interest must be direct, immediate, and not remote in consequence. A "substantial interest" is one that surpasses the common interest of all citizens.

3. Subjects that may be addressed in declaratory opinions.

The Agency will issue declaratory opinions regarding subject matters that are within the primary administrative responsibility of the Agency. Subject matters within the oversight of the Agency include the applicability of specified facts to a statute administered or enforced by the Agency or a rule promulgated by the Commission or Commissioner. The Agency will not issue a declaratory opinion regarding a statute or rule beyond the administration of the Agency.

4. Circumstances in which declaratory opinions will not be issued.

The Agency may, for good cause, refuse to issue a declaratory opinion. Without limiting the generality of the foregoing, the circumstances in which declaratory opinions will not be issued include, but are not necessarily limited to:

a. The matter is outside the primary jurisdiction of the Agency.

b. The question presented lacks clarity, the facts provided are nonsufficient to provide a conclusive determination, or the information is too vague or too broad to provide an answer.

c. A pending or active audit, criminal tax investigation, anticipated litigation, administrative action, or other determination before the Agency or court which may either answer the question presented or otherwise make an answer unnecessary on subject matter under question is in progress.
d. The statute, rule, or order on which a declaratory opinion is sought is clear and not in need of interpretation to answer the question presented.
e. The confidentiality waiver on the Declaratory Opinion Transmittal Form is not signed and provided to the Agency with the request for a declaratory opinion.
f. The request fails to contain information required by these rules or the requestor failed to follow the procedure set forth in this rule.
g. The request seeks to resolve issues that have become moot, are abstract, or involve multiple hypotheticals such that the requestor is not substantially affected by the rule or statute on which a declaratory opinion is sought.
h. No controversy exists concerning the issue as the requestor is not faced with existing facts or those certain to arise which raise a question concerning the application of the statute or rule.
i. The question presented by the request concerns the legal validity of a statute or rule.
j. The requesting party is not directly affected by the application of the statute, rule or regulation.
k. No clear answer is determinable.
l. The question presented involves the application of a criminal statute or facts that may constitute a crime.
m. The answer to the question presented would require the disclosure of information that is privileged or otherwise protected by law from disclosure.
n. The request involves an issue that may adversely affect the interests of the State, the Commission, or any of the Agency's officers or employees in any litigation that is pending or may reasonably be expected to arise.

5. Form of the request for a declaratory opinion.

a. A written request for a Declaratory Opinion, including a completed Declaratory Opinion Transmittal Form, is required. Each request must be printed or typewritten, or must be in legible handwriting. Each request must be submitted on standard business letter-size paper. Requests may be in the form of a letter addressed to the Commission Secretary or in the form of a pleading as might be addressed to a court.

b. All requests must be mailed or delivered to the Commission Secretary. The request and any envelope shall clearly state that it is a request for a declaratory opinion. Oral, telephone, or facsimile requests are not acceptable. The request must include a completed transmittal form as prescribed by the Commissioner and executed confidentiality waiver signed by the taxpayer or person requesting the declaratory opinion.

c. Each request must include the full name, telephone number, and mailing address of the requestor. All requests shall be signed by the person filing the request or a duly authorized representative. The signing party shall attest that the request complies with the requirements set forth in these rules. A declaratory opinion will have no effect if it is later determined the request did not comply with the requirements of this rule.

d. A request must be limited to a single set of facts and each request shall contain the following:

   i. Clear identification of the statute, rule, or order at issue;

   ii. Concise statement of the issue or question presented for the declaratory opinion;

   iii. Complete and accurate statement of all facts relevant to a resolution of the question presented;

   iv. Identity of all known persons involved or impacted by the factual situation causing the request, including their relationship to the facts, name, mailing address, and telephone number;

   v. Statement sufficient to show that the person seeking relief is substantially affected by the statute, rule, or regulation.

e. A request may contain relevant information to support a position or proposed opinion suggested by the requestor.

The argument may be submitted in the form of a brief containing a full discussion of the reasons, including any legal authorities in support of such position of the requestor.

f. The Agency may request that additional information be submitted by any interested party.

6. Time for Mississippi State Tax Commission's response.
   a. Within forty-five (45) days after the receipt of a request for a declaratory opinion which complies with the requirements of these rules, the Agency will respond in writing by one of the following:
      i. Issue an opinion declaring the applicability of the specified statute, rule, or order to the specified circumstances;
      ii. Decline to issue a declaratory opinion, stating the reasons for its action;
      iii. Agree to issue a declaratory opinion or a written decision declining to issue an opinion by a specified time but no later than ninety (90) days after receipt of the written request.
      iv. The forty-five (45) day period will begin on the first State of Mississippi business day after the request is received by the Agency.
   b. Responses may be sent to the authorized representative in lieu of the requesting party or the person signing the request.
7. Public availability of requests and declaratory opinions.

   Declaratory opinions and requests for declaratory opinions are available for public inspection. The taxpayer must sign a confidentiality waiver to authorize the Agency to disclose the contents of the declaratory opinion.

109 Address Information

The following are mailing and delivery addresses for correspondence with the Agency as referred to in this regulation.

1. Commission Secretary
   a. By mail: Commission Secretary, P. O. Box 22805, Jackson MS 39225-2805.
   b. By delivery: Commission Secretary, 1577 Springridge Road, Raymond MS 39154
   c. E-Mail: CommSec@mstc.state.ms.us

2. Chairman of Review Board.
   a. By mail: Chairman of Review Board, P. O. Box 22828, Jackson, MS 39225
   b. By delivery: Chairman of Review Board, 1577 Springridge Road, Raymond MS 39154
   c. E-Mail: ReviewBd@mstc.state.ms.us
3. Website.
   www.mstc.state.ms.us

110 Effective Date of Regulation

This regulation shall be in effect on and after June 30, 2005.

111 (Reserved)

112 (Reserved)

113 (Reserved)

114 (Reserved)

115 (Reserved)

116 (Reserved)

117 (Reserved)

118 (Reserved)

119 (Reserved)

120 (Reserved)

**ADOPTED BY MISSISSIPPI STATE TAX COMMISSION, APRIL 27, 2005**

*Joseph L. Blount, Commissioner of Revenue*
*Terry L. Jordan, Associate Commissioner*
*Donald L. Green, Associate Commissioner*

**ADOPTED BY CHAIRMAN, MISSISSIPPI STATE TAX COMMISSION, APRIL 27, 2005**

*Joseph L. Blount, Chairman*

**Chapter 02 Electronic Funds Transfer**

100 Scope of Rules

This chapter sets forth the rule to be used by the Mississippi State Tax Commission in the administration of Mississippi Code 27-3-81, authorizing the Mississippi State Tax Commission to require certain taxpayers to remit taxes by electronic transfer of funds so that the funds will be immediately available to the State Treasury on the due date of payment. If there is a conflict between this rule and any other rules applicable to taxes subject to electronic funds transfer, this rule shall govern.

101 Definitions

The terms and phases used in this rule shall have the meanings prescribed in this section, unless a different meaning is clearly indicated by the context in which the term or phrase is used.

1. ACH--Automated Clearing House
2. ACH Credit -- The electronic funds transfer payment method where transactions are initiated and generated by the taxpayer, cleared through the ACH system for deposit to the State Treasury.
3. ACH Debit -- The electronic funds transfer payment method where transactions are generated by the State Tax Commission upon the taxpayer's instruction and cleared through the ACH system for deposit to the State Treasury.
4. ACH Trace Number -- The unique number assigned to an electronic payment transaction by the financial institution originating the transaction.

5. Addenda Record -- The information required by the Mississippi State Tax Commission in an ACH Credit transfer or Fedwire transfer, in approved electronic format.
6. Access Code -- A confidential code assigned to each taxpayer which uniquely identifies the payor and allows the payor to communicate payment information to the Data Collection Center. The taxpayer may be given a separate access code for each tax type.
7. Automated Clearing House -- A central distribution and settlement point for the electronic clearing of debits and credits between financial institutions rather than the physical movement of paper items.
8. Call-in Day -- The day on which a taxpayer communicates payment information to the Data Collection Center.
9. Call-in Period -- The specified time interval in each call-in day during which EFT payment information received by the Data Collection Center is processed for transactions occurring on the next business day. Payment information must be communicated to the Data Collection Center prior to 3:30 p.m. (Central Time) on the call-in day to clear the ACH for deposit in the State Treasury on the next business day.
10. Confidential Taxpayer Identification Number -- See definition for access code
11. Data Collection Center -- The third party vendor who collects and processes EFT payment information from taxpayers, when using the ACH Debit method.
12. Due Date -- The date on or before which a payment is required to be made by a taxpayer under a revenue law of this state.
13. Effective Date of Implementation -- The date which the taxpayer is approved by the State Tax commission to pay a tax type using EFT.
14. EFT - Electronic Funds Transfer
15. Electronic Funds Transfer -- Any transfer of funds initiated through an electronic terminal, telephone instrument, computer or magnetic tape so as to order, instruct, or authorize a financial institution to debit or credit an account using the methods specified in this rule.
16. Fedwire -- See definition for wire transfer.

17. Mississippi Electronic Funds Transfer System -- See definition of Data Collection Center.
18. Payment Information -- The data which the Mississippi State Tax Commission requires of a taxpayer making an EFT payment.
19. Payor -- The taxpayer.
20. Reference Number -- The unique number assigned to an electronic payment transaction by the financial institution originating the transaction.
21. State Tax Commission -- The Mississippi State Tax Commission.
22. State Treasury -- The Treasury of the State of Mississippi.
23. State's Fiscal Year -- July 1 through June 30.
24. Tax Commission -- The Mississippi State Tax Commission.
25. Tax Type -- A tax, fee, license or other obligation which is subject to the EFT payment requirements, each of which shall be considered a separate category of payment. This will include all taxes, fees, licenses or other obligations which are administrated by the Mississippi Code of 1972.
26. Taxpayer -- Any person required to remit an amount to the Mississippi State Tax Commission whether it is for a tax, fee, license, or any other obligation. For the purpose of this rule, "person" includes any individual, firm, association, corporation, estate, trust, business trust, receiver, syndicate, or other group or combination acting as a unit, and includes the plural as well as the singular number.
27. Treasury -- The Treasury of the State of Mississippi.
28. Verification Code -- Code calculated from the payment amount used to ensure that the payment is communicated correctly.
29. Wire Transfer -- An instantaneous electronic funds generated by the taxpayer to the State Treasury.

102 General Requirements

1. Under the authority granted to the Mississippi State Tax Commission under Mississippi Code 27-3-81, the Mississippi State Tax Commission may require consistent with the cash management policies of the State Treasurer, that any person owing $20,000.00 or more in connection with any return,

report, or other document to be filed with the commission, can be required to remit any such tax liability by electronic funds transfer.

2. Effective January 1, 1994, the Mississippi State Tax Commission will implement an EFT program which will require certain taxpayers subject to the following taxes to remit tax payments by electronic funds transfer:
   a. Gaming
   b. Insurance Premium
   c. Beer Excise
   d. Timber Severance
   e. Tobacco Wholesale
   f. Oil Severance
   g. Gas Severance
3. The Mississippi State Tax Commission will periodically make a determination of additional tax types to be added to the EFT program. Threshold amounts will be established at that time to determine if payments made by a taxpayer subject the taxpayer to the EFT tax payment program.
4. The Mississippi State Tax Commission will make an annual determination of those taxpayers who will be required to pay a tax electronically based on prior year payment thresholds. The determination as to which taxpayers shall be subject to the remittance provisions of this rule is made by the Mississippi State Tax Commission, on a tax type by tax type basis, and is based on annual payments made to the State Tax Commission during a calendar year.
5. All taxpayers selected for the EFT program shall participate for a minimum of one year. Persons selected on the basis of prior year tax payments will be contacted by the Mississippi State Tax Commission at their last address of record. Once selected for the EFT requirement, the taxpayer must electronically transmit all payments for that tax type as provided in this rule. The Mississippi State Tax Commission will also review payments on an interim basis to identify additional taxpayers who will be required to make payments in accordance with the procedures stated in this rule.

6. The State Tax Commission will provide the selected taxpayers with forms necessary for registering to make payments for the taxes through EFT. The State Tax Commission will provide the taxpayers with instructions and procedures for paying the taxes through EFT.
7. The State Tax Commission will provide technical assistance and guidance to the taxpayers concerning the payment of taxes through EFT. An EFT hotline will be available to the taxpayers from 8:00 a.m. through 5:00 p.m. (Central Standard Time) each business day, with the exception of state holidays.

103 Selection of Taxpayers

1. On an annual basis, the State Tax Commission will review the most recent twelve month period of payment history for a taxpayer, on a tax type by tax type basis, to determine if the payment history requires the taxpayer to make payments for the tax type using EFT. If the taxpayer was not previously required to make payments for the tax type using EFT, a determination will be made as to whether the taxpayer should be required to make payments for the tax type using EFT. If the taxpayer was previously required to make payments for the tax type using EFT, a determination will be made as to whether the taxpayer should continue to be required to make payments for the tax type using EFT.
2. On an interim basis, the State Tax Commission will review payment transactions, on a tax type by tax type basis, to identify those transactions which equal or exceed the threshold amount. Taxpayers who were not previously selected as being required to make payments for a tax type using EFT and who make payments in amounts equal to or in excess of the threshold amount will be required to use EFT for the tax type.

104 Notification of Taxpayers

1. Prior to the date of the first required payment, the State Tax Commission will mail a written notice to all taxpayers selected in the annual review of transactions informing them that they are required to make payments for a tax type using EFT. The notice will identify the tax types to be paid using EFT; will provide

instructions pertaining to the payment methods available to the taxpayer; and will provide the taxpayer with the form "Registration Application For Electronic Funds Transfer."

2. The taxpayer will be required to return a properly and fully completed registration application to the State Tax Commission for each tax type the taxpayer was selected to pay using EFT or will provide a written statement explaining the reason the taxpayer should be exempted from the requirement to make payments for a tax type using EFT. The taxpayer will use the registration application to make an election as to which payment method the taxpayer will use. A taxpayer who elects to use the ACH Credit payment method in lieu of the ACH Debit payment method must file a written request with the registration application to use the ACH Credit method. The request must state the reason for requesting the ACH Credit payment method.

*Courtesy of Louis G. Fuller, Brunini, Grantham, Grower & Hewes PLLC*

## Appendix C

## ADMINISTRATIVE APPEALS

**§ 27-77-5. Appeals from commission actions; appeal must be in writing; notice and hearing; appeal to commission from decision of board of review; hearing before commission; withdrawal of appeal.**

(1) Any taxpayer aggrieved by an assessment of tax by the agency, by the agency's denial of a refund claim, or by the denial of a waiver of tag penalty, and who wishes to contest the action of the agency shall, within thirty (30) days from the date of the action, file an appeal in writing with the board of review requesting a hearing and correction of the contested action specifying in detail the relief requested and any other information that might be required by regulation.

(2) Upon receipt of a timely written appeal from a tax assessment, refund claim denial or denial of waiver of a tag penalty, a hearing shall be scheduled before the board of review unless it is determined that the relief requested in the written appeal should be granted without a hearing. A notice of the hearing shall be mailed to the taxpayer advising the taxpayer of the date, time and location of the hearing. The taxpayer or his designated representative shall attend the hearing unless a request is made to, and granted by, the board of review to allow the taxpayer to submit his position in writing or by electronic transmission in lieu of attendance. Failure of the taxpayer or his designated representative to attend a hearing or to submit his position in writing or by electronic transmission by the date specified by the board of review or by the hearing date, if no date was specified, shall constitute a withdrawal of the appeal.

(3) At a hearing before the board of review on a tax assessment, denial of refund claim, or denial of waiver of a tag penalty, the board of review shall try the issues presented, according to law and the facts and within the guidelines established by regulation. The hearing before the board of review shall be informal and no official transcript will be made of the hearing. At the earliest practical date after the hearing, the members of the board of review that heard the appeal shall make a determination on the matter

presented and notify the taxpayer of its findings by mailing a copy of its order to the taxpayer. If the order involves the appeal of a denial of a waiver of tag penalty, a copy of the order shall also be mailed to the tax collector that imposed the penalty. If in the order the board of review orders the taxpayer to pay a tax assessment, the taxpayer shall, within thirty (30) days from the date of the order, pay the amount ordered to be paid or appeal the order of the board of review to the commission. After the thirty-day period, if the tax determined by the board of review to be due is not paid and an appeal from the order of the board of review is not made to the commission, the agency shall proceed to collect the tax assessment as determined by the board of review.

(4) Any taxpayer aggrieved by an order of the board of review affirming a tax assessment, the denial of a refund claim, or the denial of a waiver of tag penalty, and who wishes to contest the order shall, within thirty (30) days from the date of the order of the board of review being contested, file an appeal to the commission. The appeal shall be in writing and shall request a hearing and reversal or modification of the order of the board of review, specify in detail the relief requested and contain any other information that might be required by regulation, and be filed with the commission secretary. Failure to timely file a written appeal with the commission secretary within the thirty-day period shall make the order of the board of review final and not subject to further review by the commission or a court, other than as to the issue of whether a written appeal from the order of the board of review was timely filed with the commission secretary.

(5) Upon receipt of a written appeal from an order of the board of review affirming a tax assessment, refund claim denial or denial of waiver of a tag penalty, the commission secretary shall schedule a hearing before the commission on the appeal. A notice of this hearing shall be mailed to the taxpayer advising the taxpayer of the date, time and location of hearing. The taxpayer or his designated representative shall attend the hearing unless a request is made to and granted by the commission to allow the taxpayer to submit his position in writing or by electronic transmission in lieu of attendance. Failure of the taxpayer or his designated representative to attend a hearing or to submit his position in writing or by electronic transmission by the date specified by the commission or by the hearing date, if no date was specified, shall constitute a withdrawal of the appeal.

(6) At any hearing before the commission on an appeal of an order of the board of review affirming a tax assessment, refund claim denial or denial of waiver of a tag penalty, two (2) members of the commission shall constitute a quorum. At the hearing, the commission shall try the issues presented, according to the law and the facts and pursuant to any guidelines established by regulation. The rules of evidence shall be relaxed at the hearing. Any appeal to chancery court from an order of the commission resulting from this type of hearing shall include a full evidentiary judicial hearing on the issues presented. No official transcript shall be made of this hearing before the commission. After reaching a decision on the issues presented, the commission shall enter its order setting forth its findings and decision on the appeal. A copy of the order of the commission shall be mailed to the taxpayer. If the order involves an appeal of a denial of a waiver of tag penalty, a copy of the order shall also be mailed to the tax collector that imposed the penalty.

(7) If in its order the commission orders a taxpayer to pay a tax assessment, the taxpayer shall, within thirty (30) days from the date of the order, pay the amount ordered to be paid or properly appeal said order of the commission to chancery court as provided in Section 27-77-7. After the thirty-day period, if the tax determined by the commission to be due is not paid and an appeal from the commission order has not been properly filed, the agency shall proceed to collect the tax assessment as affirmed by the commission. If in its order the commission determines that the taxpayer has overpaid his taxes, the agency shall refund or credit to the taxpayer, as provided by law, the amount of overpayment as determined and set out in the order.

(8) At any time after the filing of an appeal to the board of review or from the board of review to the commission under this section, an appeal can be withdrawn. Such a withdrawal of an appeal may be made voluntarily by the taxpayer or may occur involuntarily as a result the taxpayer failing to appear at a scheduled hearing, failing to make a written submission or electronic transmission in lieu of attendance at a hearing by the date specified or by the hearing date, if no date was specified, or by any other act or failure that the board of review or the commission determines represents a failure on the part of the taxpayer to prosecute his appeal. Any voluntary withdrawal shall be in writing or by electronic transmission and sent by the taxpayer or

his designated representative to the chairman of the board of review, if the appeal being withdrawn is to the board of review, or to the commission secretary, if the appeal being withdrawn is to the commission. If the withdrawal of appeal is involuntary, the administrative appeal body from whom the appeal is being withdrawn shall note on its minutes the involuntary withdrawal of the appeal and the basis for the withdrawal. Once an appeal is withdrawn, whether voluntary or involuntary, the action from which the appeal was taken, whether a tax assessment, a denial of refund claim, a denial of waiver of tax penalty, or an order of the board of review, shall become final and not subject to further review by the board of review, the commission or a court. The agency shall then proceed in accordance with law based on such final action.

(9) Nothing in this section shall bar a taxpayer from timely applying to the commissioner as otherwise provided by law for a tax refund or for a revision in tax.

**Sources:** Laws, 2005, ch. 499, § 3, eff from and after July 1, 2005.

*Courtesy of Louis G. Fuller, Brunini, Grantham, Grower & Hewes PLLC*

## Appendix D

## JUDICIAL REVIEW

**§ 27-77-7. Judicial review of commission's findings and order; petition; surety bond; payment under protest in lieu of bond; issuance of summons; trial; appeals of chancery court order to Supreme Court.**

(1) The findings and order of the commission entered under Section 27-77-5 shall be final unless the taxpayer shall, within thirty (30) days from the date of the order, file a petition in the chancery court appealing the order and pay the tax or post the bond as required in this chapter. The petition shall be filed against the State Tax Commission and shall contain a concise statement of the facts as contended by the taxpayer, identify the order from which the appeal is being taken and set out the type of relief sought. If in the action, the taxpayer is seeking a refund or credit for an alleged overpayment of tax or for taxes paid in protest under subsection (3) of this section, the taxpayer shall allege in the petition that he alone bore the burden of the tax sought to be refunded or credited and did not directly or indirectly collect the tax from anyone else.

(2) A petition under subsection (1) of this section shall be filed in the chancery court of the county or judicial district in which the taxpayer has a place of business or in the Chancery Court of the First Judicial District of Hinds County, Mississippi; however, a resident taxpayer may file the petition in the chancery court of the county or judicial district in which he is a resident.

(3) A petition filed under subsection (1) of this section that appeals an order of the commission affirming a tax assessment, shall be accompanied by a surety bond approved by the clerk of the court in a sum double the amount in controversy, conditioned to pay the judgment of the court. The clerk shall not approve a bond unless the bond is issued by a surety company qualified to write surety bonds in this state. As an alternative to the posting of bond, a taxpayer appealing an order of the commission affirming a tax assessment may, prior to the filing of the petition, pay to the agency, under protest, the amount ordered by the commission to be paid and seek a refund of such taxes, plus interest thereon.

(4) Upon the filing of the petition under subsection (1) of this section, the clerk of the court shall issue a summons to the State Tax Commission requiring the commission to answer or otherwise respond to the petition within thirty (30) days of service. The summons shall be served on the State Tax Commission by personal service on the commissioner as the chief executive officer of the State Tax Commission. The chancery court in which a petition under subsection (1) of this section is properly filed shall have jurisdiction to hear and determine said cause or issues joined as in other cases. In any petition in which the taxpayer is seeking a refund or credit for an alleged overpayment of tax or for taxes paid under protest under subsection (3) of this section, the taxpayer shall prove by a preponderance of the evidence that he alone bore the burden of the tax sought to be refunded or credited and did not directly or indirectly collect the tax from anyone else. At trial of any action brought under this section, the chancery court shall give deference to the decision and interpretation of law and regulations by the commission as it does with the decisions and interpretation of any administrative agency, but it shall try the case de novo and conduct a full evidentiary judicial hearing on the issues raised. Based on the evidence presented at the hearing, the chancery court shall determine whether the taxpayer has proven, by a preponderance of the evidence or a higher standard if required by the issues raised, that he is entitled to any or all of the relief he has requested. The chancery court shall decide all questions presented, including those as to legality and the amount of tax or refund due, and if it finds that the tax assessment or denial of refund claim in issue is incorrect or invalid, in whole or in part, it shall determine the amount of tax or refund due, including interest and, if applicable, penalty to date, and enter such order or judgment as it deems proper. Interest and penalty included in this determination shall be computed by the court based on the methods for computing penalty and interest as specified by law for the type of tax in issue. Either the State Tax Commission or the taxpayer, or both, shall have the right to appeal from the order of the chancery court to the Supreme Court as in other cases. If an appeal is taken from the order of the chancery court, the bond provided for in subsection (3) of this section shall continue to remain in place until a final decision is rendered in the case.

**Sources:** Laws, 2005, ch. 499, § 4, eff from and after July 1, 2005.

*Courtesy of Louis G. Fuller, Brunini, Grantham, Grower & Hewes PLLC*

## Appendix E

# HOW TO REQUEST A PRIVATE LETTER RULING

Requests for private letter rulings (PLR) must be submitted in writing to:

Policy Services Division
Louisiana Department of Revenue
P O Box 44098
Baton Rouge, LA 70804-4098

Requests must be submitted by an identified taxpayer, or by the taxpayer's representative who has a power of attorney from the taxpayer. PLRs are not issued to tax practitioners who do not identify the clients for whom the rulings are sought.

Requests for PLRs must provide the following information:

- The name, address, and telephone number of the person requesting the private letter ruling;
- A power of attorney, if the person is represented by a third party;
- A statement of the specific questions to be answered or issues to be addressed in the private letter ruling;
- Citations to or copies of relevant statutes, regulations, court decisions, advisory opinions, or other authority that appear to support the position of the person requesting the ruling;
- A statement attesting:
    - Whether the person requesting the opinion has the same issue under audit or appeal with the department or with any other taxing or revenue authority;
    - If the person requesting the opinion has been notified that an examination or audit is pending;
    - If the person requesting the opinion is litigating the issues;
    - If the department, or any other taxing or revenue authority, has previously issued an advisory opinion on the

subject matter discussed in the request for the private letter ruling (with copy attached);

- If the Attorney General's Office has been, or will be, requested to issue an opinion concerning the issue, and
- That prior to the issuance of a PLR, if the requesting person is notified of a pending examination or audit by the department or other taxing or revenue authority, they will notify the Secretary of the pending examination.

*Courtesy of Jaye Calhoun, McGlinchey Stafford PLLC*